MONEY MIND

MONEY MIND

BEYOND SPECULATION

B.R. SUTTON

LIONCREST
PUBLISHING

Money Mind

Beyond Speculation

ISBN 978-1-5445-2977-6 Hardcover
      978-1-5445-2978-3 Paperback
      978-1-5445-2979-0 Ebook

I dedicate this book to my unwavering

and eternally patient partner, Nichole,

and our three incredible kids:

Kirsten, Shane, and Jackson.

CONTENTS

PREFACE

Writing a book about becoming financially free while avoiding the temptations and perils of gambling has been important to me for a long time. It's even more important now. We've reached an incredibly dangerous time in the financial cycle. Central banks are printing billions of new dollars in stimulus money to give to understimulated people who are using it to speculate on stocks and crypto on their iPhones. Those "investors" expect something for nothing, and no one seems to acknowledge the risks. No one wants to take the time to understand how their relationship with and attitude toward money will directly impact their personal experience. Everyone wants to become an investor, but no one is taking the time to learn how.

It all begins in the mind.

Like many people seeking a better life, I just wanted autonomy. I wanted to be able to make money without a boss, to be an entrepreneur without inventory or staff or meetings. I wanted something for myself to be proud of. I tried and tried, and always ended up right back where I started. That is, until I set out to learn the rules of money and set some strict guidelines for myself.

I used to joke that I wanted to be able to wake up from a coma with one hundred dollars and my MacBook, and immediately make a living for myself. And that's exactly what I've done—and what I am going to teach you.

I didn't start from a position of strength. My motivation was that I was riddled with anxiety and depression. But coming to grips early on with the idea that I was "different" was the fuel I needed to think differently, build a nest egg, and earn my own financial runway: a period of time to decide what I want to be when I grow up.

To put it another way, I wanted enough money to just *live*.

I failed miserably in my first attempts at investing. I opened a brokerage account as soon as I turned eighteen in 2002 with the dream of making it big as a day trader. With zero knowledge or guidance, I threw $1,000 into an Interactive Brokers account and turned it into zero dollars that same week. I did this about fifty times before I stopped and learned how to trade stocks. I could feel that I was somehow getting in my own way and causing myself to fail. After the collapse of Lehman Brothers sent me back to zero again in 2008, I started from scratch in the spring of 2009. This time, I not only knew how to trade; I also had some strict rules to live by. This time, I started to grow my account to the point where I was making far more than I had ever received through a paycheck or business venture. That's when I really began my journey as an independent speculator.

One thing was clear to me through those early days: I was going to *get rich or die trading*.

It took me almost until my thirtieth year—and I should have had it nailed by my twentieth. Like so many others, I suffer from being a contrarian and pessimistic investor. I allow my fearful thoughts to manifest into my portfolio: I am too bearish and cautious in a bull market, and I am too eager and opportunistic in a bear market. I sell when I should hold. I buy when I should wait. Throughout my twenties, I was breaking what became my rule number one: never let your emotions influence your decisions.

If you want to be independent, you have to start operating like a bank. And everyone knows a bank has no emotions.

In this book, I will share with you how I made millions and lost millions—and why. How I lost $1.7 million in one bad trade and how I left $25 million on the table after being the second hire at one of the biggest cannabis companies on earth—all to regain my autonomy. I still make mistakes, but now I'm able to pinpoint exactly where and when I go wrong, I'm able to accept it, pick up the pieces, and move forward stronger than before. I have seen people go into deep depressions over losses of a few thousand dollars. My aim here is to show you how to detach from that gut-wrenching feeling most people get from money—gaining it or losing it—and instead learn how to be a good host to it and a humble student of everything about it. I will teach you how to see loss as education and how to see wins as validation of your increased wisdom about finances and economics.

These days I am better able to recognize when I am making decisions from a place of intellect, intuition, and spirit rather than from one of FOMO, blind greed, or sheer restlessness.

I can recognize how my different moods and energies affect my investment decisions. Or how something as small as a hangover or smoking a joint can cause long-lasting mistakes in my online brokerage account.

These days, especially, I have learned that everyone's real superpower is eating and sleeping well, loving yourself, and avoiding the things that are not serving you or that are harming your inner peace. Making small changes in those departments will have a drastic and positive impact in your professional and financial life.

It's true that money doesn't buy you happiness. I will explain the lottery phenomenon and how I found myself going from poor and happy to rich and beyond miserable before I landed somewhere in the middle.

I did this without a high school education and with extreme ADD and number dyslexia. There is no math or number crunching involved in my methods. I'm not an advanced technical trader, nor am I a financial analyst. There's no need for any tough equations or Excel sheets.

If I can do this, you can too.

Thank you for taking care and attention toward your own personal finances and the way you perceive them. If everyone was as diligent, life would be better for all of us.

Let's begin.

INTRODUCTION

Viva Las Vegas

For a couple of years from 2016 to 2018, I was one of the largest cannabis operators in Las Vegas.

At the time, pot was legal in Nevada but illegal in the United States.

That would not have been a problem for me if I'd lived in Vegas, where we grew and sold the weed, but I lived in Canada. I left my wife and kids at home almost every week and drove to Vancouver to smuggle myself down to Sin City.

When I landed, I wasn't just entering Nevada. I was entering the United States. Every time I crossed the federal border, I became a criminal in the eyes of the US Department of Homeland Security. An affable, miniature Canadian Pablo Escobar of pot trying to cross the border.

My whole life became fixated on the gut-wrenching moments when I had to cross over. More than sixty times in two years, I walked up to the counter to hand my passport to the agent. Each time, I had to become someone else. A man with a specific reason to justify his visit, usually tickets to a local golf tournament. A man who couldn't carry a laptop or a suit for fear of suggesting he was there for business. A man who had to carry a burner phone with no pictures, no stored numbers, no call or text history.

Anyone but a Canada-based CEO whose public company sold over a million dollars' worth of high-quality weed in Vegas every month.

A single text message or email implicating me in the pot trade would get me barred from the States for life. A single Google search at the desk from the agent would do the same. It was happening to cannabis executives every day.

At the time, I was a seasoned speculator who had become an accidental investor and then an accidental executive who could not stop throwing good money after bad. I didn't know how to cut a loss and say no.

I should have stuck to the trading rules that had served me well so far. Instead, I'd gotten sucked in deeper and deeper, and things were going from bad to worse.

I didn't fit in in Vegas. Every week, I told myself it was time to quit. And every week, everyone else told me to keep going. The guys on the board wanted me to keep responsibility for the company and wouldn't interview the other candidates I suggested to take my place as CEO. The investors I had brought to the company wanted me there to watch over their investment. The 180 employees and

100 construction staff wanted me to protect their jobs. Market executives wanted me to offer them sector insight on an hourly basis.

It all went to my head and weeks became years.

I enjoyed being told by lawyers and MBAs how great I was. I loved hearing that I alone was making the enterprise a huge success. I loved the kudos after I raised $80 million in startup capital from an investment bank for this exciting new frontier, legal weed in Vegas.

It was an addictive new drug for a street kid with zero postsecondary education, let alone ninth-grade math or English. I was a drug-addicted, stressed out, high school dropout with three young kids. No wonder my ego took over. No wonder I broke my own rules when emotions ran high. I was the exact demographic that people didn't expect anything from.

I mistakenly let emotions, peer pressure, and coercion influence my decision-making.

I was in turmoil every day from fear and greed, swinging wildly back and forth between the two, from total despair to utter elation from one encounter to the next. And all of it—every call, every trip, every issue, every party—was about one thing: money. Money was the only reason for me to be there.

The pursuit of paper had led me to carry on with reckless abandon, a voracious appetite for learning, and a drive to never fail. In my rebellion, I chose the roadless path that was the emerging cannabis industry and forged a way through the uncleared landscape, blazing the trail ahead of the pack who would come after me. In many ways, I sacrificed myself for the sector. In the process, I burned the candle at both ends until I came to a place of exhaustion and emptiness, and neglected relationships with connectedness, spirit, and all the loved ones in my life.

DRUG TRADE

Thomas Jefferson could have been talking about me when he said, "I prefer dangerous freedom over peaceful slavery." I ended up in the markets because I wanted freedom and ended up in Vegas because I liked danger and took massive risks for a living. The gig fit me at the time, but I wasn't mindful of the tilt. That's what gamblers call the energizing adrenaline and confidence that comes in poker when you start to get hot hands, when winning gives you too much confidence and makes you play outside of your zone, causing you to make critical errors.

It's what Tony Soprano called "cowboyitis."

To all appearances, I was living the life, but for all the debauchery and nights out, I knew that I was spiraling emotionally and mentally. Every late night in Vegas, I said to myself, "I should not be here right now." I was a square peg in a round hole.

Although I was the opposite, I felt like an imposter. An infiltrator who had gone way too deep and wanted to pull the chute.

I was a speculator and stock trader who had zero formal training. I hadn't done an MBA at college, I hadn't trained as a stock operator, and I was never a banker, commodities trader, or stockbroker. I had never worked in the capital markets, nor had my dad, as was the case for all my peers in the stock market.

I was an expert in three limited categories—motorcycles, firearms, and cannabis—but not in the kind of illegal way that might suggest. I was in the motorbike business, and I started and owned what was, at one time, Canada's largest online firearms marketplace, as well as the medical cannabis resource, CannabisHealth.com, which kept me in close contact with medical professionals in cannabis all over the world. I started those companies because nothing like them existed in the marketplace at the time. I also taught myself how to trade in the markets from books that were almost one hundred years old.

I started working full time at age fifteen installing flooring. By nineteen, I was running an IT department for one of the world's biggest oil companies. That was when I figured out that I could make more money in a week by buying and selling shares in that company than by sitting at my desk from nine to five like some sort of obedient drone.

So I quit and made trading my job, but it was the legal weed biz that made stock trading my life.

STONE ME

When cannabis started to become legal in parts of North America, I was perfectly set to take advantage from state to state.

I'd been a consumer since the age of fourteen, and I felt I knew more about the product side than anyone. The potheads who bred and grew the weed couldn't communicate with the money guys. And the money guys couldn't communicate with the artisan gardeners.

I could relate to both sides. I understood the industry intimately from the top down. I understood the customers and their habits. I understood the nuances of the trade from being in the room since the nineties. I knew where the value was, I knew how to vet operators and financial models, and most importantly, I knew what drove the behavioral economics of an industry that's really hard to pin down or predict because it's in a constant state of evolution. Sometimes we are most dangerous in fields that are right under our nose: it's important to be a true subject-matter expert in the field in which you derive your income.

"Do what you love" is useless advice, as most people are not good earners in their fields of passion. Do what you're *good at*, and the fulfillment and money will follow.

My sensitivity and intuition were strengths. My curiosity and empathy were strengths. My pessimism was a strength. My distrust was a strength. I was known for having the best nose for bullshit in the business. I was the guy the industry shot-callers would parachute into battle to gather intel and report back. I was hired by global leaders like Marc Lustig, respected analysts like Alan Brochstein, and penny-stock cowboys like Terry Booth. The top early names in the biz hired me to be their eyes and ears on the street in 2014 as everyone jockeyed for position.

I took the advice of Ray Dalio, who runs one of the largest hedge funds in the world. When asked the secret of his success, Dalio said, "I say *no* 99.9 percent of the time. That's it. I see great stuff all day. I say no to it all day."

I realized that Dalio and people like him live by hard and fast rules, so I started to do the same. That gained me a following on Twitter in 2008 and 2009, and people started to ask my opinion about this trade or that opportunity. I spent much of those years warning everyone that most of the early pot stocks were literal scams. MJNA and PHOT were the only two options at the time, and both were illiquid startup companies with over a billion shares outstanding on the OTC, trading far below one penny but telling prospective investors with a straight face, "We'll be a dollar next year."

I made a name for being able to call those guys out and also for being able to find value, which is how I wound up running a $200 million public corporation in Canada with more than 38,000 shareholders at the peak of the cannabis mania. They were the same people I had put in Supreme Cannabis, where I was the Executive VP from inception some three years earlier; then Aurora Cannabis, where I was the Director of Business Development and the first capital markets hire in 2014; and then Origin House, where I assisted with the go-public and trading side of things, as well as the early M&A in 2015–2016. I speculated on the legalized cannabis industry, riding the wave and blazing new trails each and every quarter, and having the time of my life because I was one of the rare subject-matter experts. I had been involved early in the legal weed trade in Colorado and Washington in 2012, then California and Nevada in 2016.

But Nevada had gone wrong. The investors had sent me in to save the company, but I knew even before I arrived that the investment was dead. Too many politicians, legacy owners, promoters, and industry operators all had their hand in the cookie jar. Worse yet, 9 percent of the license still belonged to the original founders, and I knew it was a fatal error not having a clean corporate structure. We had break-ins, things went missing daily, and it was a generally sketchy situation at the best of times, with everyone in management demanding more pay every month as revenue increased.

I had people driving upward of $500,000 every Friday to a bank in downtown Las Vegas and trying to explain the nuances of our legal operation and why the teller should just take the cash and shut up. I had people driving bags of cash to the IRS office every month. We all had to do retinal scans and fingerprints with the FBI annually to maintain our "agent card" to grow, sell, and transport cannabis in Clark County. We even had a corporate Canadian bank account holding over $18 million in cash raised through Canaccord Genuity get closed on us, giving me only seven days to move the funds elsewhere at a time when not one bank in the country would take business from legal cannabis operators—let alone $18,000,000 in cash.

It was plate spinning on a whole new level. It was hell.

Every day I felt like as soon as I stopped holding it all together, the game would be up. Which, by the way, is exactly what happened. A final threat of "consequences if you don't pay" from a New York–based wannabe mobster masquerading as a hedge fund manager, who was shaking us down for a huge monthly retainer, helped me make my decision that it was finally time to quit the mayhem. The little Vegas company was worth $200 million and had over $20 million in cash, but it had too many mouths to feed to make it all work. Within six months of the locals taking over corporate and operations, it was worth $30 million, and cash on hand was a measly $2 million. It had been pillaged by the vultures as soon as those who cared left.

Months after I quit, the company was a shell of what it had been. It had been primarily my efforts and my continual fundraising and stock stimulation that had kept the company going. Much of the growth was at my expense, as I was always far and away the biggest buyer of the company's stock on the open market. I was the jockey that whipped the horse into shape every day, an important lesson on "bet on the jockey, not the horse." The founding investors were right to put me in control: I cared way too much. I owned every problem. No one else could care about them or our other shareholders as much as I did. I wore it every day. I was the guy that was supposed to die on his sword, if need be. I was the only guy willing to put every last penny he had into the stock with the long-term vision in mind.

It turned out I was all alone. The company went from licensing deals with Tony Hawk, DNA Genetics, and Jack Herer in 2018 to selling infused joints in Vegas for LA rappers Kurupt and Daz into a shell of what it once was, laying off all the critical people in an effort to survive the "vape crisis" of 2019 and then later the coronavirus lockdowns in 2020.

My experience in Las Vegas is an object lesson for what can go wrong for people who want to play the markets: stocks, crypto, commodities, or anything else. It's a metaphor for how the whole trading system is set up to work against the little guy. The big boys don't want you there other than to offer them some liquidity. And they will make it as difficult as possible because they want to ensure that they win and that you lose.

I was already a successful speculator, but I still screwed up. I learned hard lessons after going against my own set of rules. I could have stayed retired and said no to Vegas and enjoyed three leisurely years of growth and no headaches, but I didn't because I was unable to recognize at the time that emotion was driving the bus.

Anyone who wants to thrive as an independent trader can learn from what happened to me without having to go through it. My experience was extreme, but most people who trade any type of financial instruments for themselves have been through something similar—white-knuckling their way through the week, watching quotes go up and down, watching the numbers on the screen flicker, throwing good money at a trade that's already gone bad. Remember this when your favorite e-gaming company or crypto startup asks you to "join them." They're asking you to save them.

If you're an adventurer like me, you've already experienced the addictive thrill of success: the appeal to emotion, ego, and, frankly, greed. Or maybe anticipating that thrill is what's tempting you to try your hand at trading stock. And if you're like me, you've probably shared the same devastating feelings of loss when things go wrong, spiral out of control, flicker from green to red, then red, red, red . . .

It doesn't have to be that way.

HOW TO BE A SWASHBUCKLER

Vegas weed wasn't my only trade that had gone bad, but it had the most drastic consequences and fucked up a solid three years of my life. It affected my health, my friends, and my family. I walked away far less happy and with a lower net worth. You could call it the cost of tuition.

Losing money is an unavoidable part of trading. Losing your sanity shouldn't be.

Nor should losing your independence or your autonomy, which was what hurt me the most.

I pride myself on being an independent foot soldier in the markets. A swashbuckler. I've never had a boss or a client telling me what to buy or sell. I've never had a broker picking stocks on my behalf.

I study the markets for myself, make my own decisions, and place my own trades. That's how I started out, and it's how I still operate. It's how everyone could operate with a little help and encouragement.

I started trading mainly because I had so many brutal jobs and horrible bosses from the age of fourteen, and I didn't want to do it anymore. I didn't want to work a job for thirty or forty years, get to the age of sixty, and have regrets.

That fear was the fuel that made me want to be a professional speculator. I needed to be 100 percent independent. More specifically, I needed to not be dependent on anyone, any job, trade, source of income, or anything else. I *needed* autonomy.

I decided to stop trading my time for money and turned my checkbook into my tool belt. Every book I read told me to take the little money I had and put it to work. I didn't know how to do it, but everyone said the same thing: put your money to work for you.

Don't trade your time for money because money is the most abundant commodity in the world, and time is the most finite.

When I set out, my definition of success was to be able to wake up, open my laptop, and make a couple of hundred bucks independently of anyone else in the world using my own money in my own portfolio with no calls to agents, brokers, or market scallywags. My phone pinged at 9:15 a.m. every day with the same calendar message: "Make 300 bucks today, smile, and have gratitude."

The target went up over time, but every day when I hit it, I closed my laptop and went mountain biking, visited friends, and spent time with my wife and kids. My goal was simple: no office, no boss, no meetings, no calls, no stupid outfits, no inventory, and no fucking around waiting on others. Just me, my online brokerage account, and the world markets.

In this book, I'm going to show you how. And you don't have to sell yourself out in Vegas to do it. You don't need to be a financial genius or a math whiz. You don't need to start with a fortune. You don't need a crystal ball or the power of prayer.

You need common sense and a set of rules to trade by. Above all, you need to understand yourself, why you are trading, and what you count as success. You need to know when to recognize that you've made it, and you need to learn how to enjoy the process.

Being an independent trader isn't a short cut to success. It's actually one of the hardest ways to make a living. But making money isn't the main problem with trading.

Cutting through the noise and bullshit, internal and external, is the problem. Understanding yourself and having clear and defined goals is the problem. Having enough discipline to stick to the rules is the problem.

To this day, I find myself constantly journaling and reflecting every time I want to break away from my plan in midflight. I need constant reminders and tools to help me. I create friction points, and I hold myself accountable.

In this book, I'm going to show you how those rules made it possible for me to thrive as an independent despite the vast forces ranged against me—and against you.

One thing most new traders never consider is this: the markets don't exist to make you money. They exist to part suckers from their money. Period. Those digits on the screen only keep blinking green because people like you are pumping money into the markets and licking their wounds as it vanishes, sucked into the frenzy of flashing lights like a pensioner at a slot machine.

It's not a victimless sport. Your success is someone else's failure. The people who started the market machine did so to make money for themselves—to transfer wealth from your family to theirs. Ordinary people don't own stocks. The system is set up to benefit the wealthy and the insiders. That's why 50 percent of all stock owned by American households is held by 1 percent of Americans.

But that's starting to change in our new world. You might not be an insider, but the good news is that you don't have to be a sucker like our parents and their parents before them.

I'm proof that independents can break in and play the system from the inside. And if I can do it without as much as a high school diploma, then anyone can.

I grew up feeling out of place wherever I was. I'd been thrown out of kindergarten at five years old for failing to obey and have been bullied my entire life. I watched alcoholism kill my father a week after I turned twenty. My mom's mental illness made her reject my brother and me from birth. She sent me to live with women in the church from the age of one, and later sent me to fringe Christian schools in thrift-store clothes to receive an education she constantly reminded me was worthless. She drove home the point every day that the world is out to get you, so trust no one and question everything. After attending more than ten schools and living in fifteen different homes before I turned fifteen, I dropped out without finishing ninth grade. I was a homeless drug addict before my fifteenth birthday. My odds of a good outcome were near zero.

I was lucky I didn't know that at the time.

After my dad died, I had no mentors or male figures to look up to. I had to ask for advice and seek mentorship in creative ways. When I was twenty-three, I managed a sales department at a Harley-Davidson dealership and sought advice from wealthy businessmen, gangsters, and cops. They were the only ones who would walk in and buy a $45,000 Road Glide on a Tuesday afternoon when everyone else was at work trying to make ends meet, so I figured they had to know something about making money. It turned out in that case that those three demographics simply used debt to fuel their egos and squash their insecurities. That was a big lesson in asset allocation, leverage, risk mitigation, and stupid ego-driven impulse purchases.

Before I turned thirty, I'd become a multimillionaire by playing the markets and studying all of God's bizarre creatures and how they earned and spent their money.

That's why I say, if I can do it, anyone can. It's a question of mindset. Of desire and discipline.

Stop Chasing Money; Chase Satisfaction

Realize that you're only thirty days from freedom. If you hate your life because you hate your job or your income level, you *can* do something about it.

Figure out what you actually want to do—and what's stopping you from doing it. And then just do it.

Yes, finance and business books will help you immensely get over the learning curve. It's how I taught myself to trade. In his book *Shoe Dog* (2016), Phil Knight, the founder of Nike, says over and over, "Just start doing it." Start doing it shitty and get better with time.

If you wait until you're great, you'll never begin.

Figure out what you want to do, what you could be really good at, and start doing it today. Time is too precious to waste another day.

This book will give you some tools. It will share the rules I use and teach you some of the lessons I've learned from studying the leading thinkers in the money game. But it only works if you go do it—if you apply it in your own life. No one can do this for you. No one cares about your money and your success as much as you do.

That's what I did. When I quit my last job, my goal was to become a pro trader, so I started trading. But here's the thing. If I had waited to start trading until I thought I was perfect, I never would have started.

"Don't Do Nothing" Is Not the Same as Saying, "Be Reckless"

You don't start out by betting the farm. It could be a $7,000 trade or a $70,000 trade. You approach it the same as you would a $7 million transaction, which is, by the way, only two digits away and, in many cases, is actually less work and has fewer moving parts.

You have to stop thinking, "That's too big for me. I can't buy into that."

You "buy the suit for the job you want," not the one you have. You start by acting the part, then you grow into it, like Oprah or Kid Rock or any other high achiever with humble beginnings. They all started out as unknown amateurs, cringy rookies. So choose a role that gives you fulfillment, and start playing it: trader, investor, angel investor, financier, philanthropist. Decide what role to assume: you can be anything you want to be.

I decided to play the role of a portfolio manager, which is a job that usually requires an MBA and CFA designation, which is one of the hardest designations to get.

Needless to say, I don't have either.

So I started playing the role of *my own* portfolio manager, and I became the real thing. Now I have investments all over the world in everything from battery metals and silver mining to uranium exploration, psychedelic therapy, blockchain and DeFi startups, health devices, fintech, alternative protein sources, clean tech, ESG, water, e-gaming, media, online education, and more.

I own a small part of about a hundred companies—a situation I always thought would have taken me many more decades to get to.

That's one of the lessons I absorbed from all those old books on self-improvement (some of which, by the way, were written by men with similar backgrounds to my own, just as some of Canada's leading billionaires are the children of poverty-stricken immigrants or are people who struggle with mental health issues who never went to college). You can stop being who you are now today; you can become whatever you want to be. A significant number of the world's billionaires are also dyslexic and children of addicts.

SELF-CONTROL

I got hooked on trading the same way I got hooked on everything else. Money, or the pursuit of it, can be a dangerous addiction, and it needs to be managed like any other.

There are many parallels between the drug trade and the investment trade, but the main one is that they are both working against you, the user. They are set up to keep you hooked as quickly as possible, to take your cash with no regard for your well-being. They both deliver short-term gratification at the cost of thinking about the long-term consequences: "Borrowing happiness from tomorrow." They both seem to offer an upward path to something better, something more fun, but they can both quickly lead you down to the bottom of a very deep hole. A hole that gets harder to climb out of the deeper you dig it.

It's time to drop the shovel and stop digging.

Trading is like any other addiction, but the rules allow you to control it. They help you keep away from the pitfalls and blind spots so you can spot opportunities and learn when to step forward with conviction and learn when to walk away with no regrets. You can approach the market with the confidence and discipline of the people on the inside. You can see through the smoke and mirrors. And you can do it all from home without ever working for anyone else or paying your hard-earned cash to charlatans, hucksters, boosters, scammers, con men, frauds, false prophets, desperate CEOs, outright thieves, and even accredited financial advisors—who are determined to sell you information or services you don't need so that they can pay their rent this month. If a broker didn't need your money, he would be an investor. He wouldn't need other people's assets to carve out income for himself.

You're stepping into a circus that welcomes clowns. "Come on in, idiot! Welcome! Take a seat! Can I get you a coffee? Did you hear today's news?"

Every now and then in the economic cycle, the market opens up, and everyone wants to be involved. We're going through a phase like that now unlike any we have ever seen before. This is so much bigger than 1929, than 1987, than the tech bubble of 2000, or the financial crisis of 2008.

Welcome to the "everything bubble."

Cheap and abundant credit has made a buyer out of everyone. Everything is experiencing a sellers' market, where qualified buyers are lined up down the street, but inventory is low across the board and freight is backed up, so prices keep going up...and will continue to do so. It's about to get much worse if governments don't raise interest rates to get everyone off the cheap booze, the open bar of easy, low-cost money. When assets like real estate or goods like groceries keep going up every year, it means that either hyperinflation is approaching or that when gravity eventually kicks in, in the form of a reset, the burst of the bubble will be a biblical event, causing catastrophic loss across all asset classes.

It's worth remembering the old joke from the time of the Depression. "When the doorman of the building is giving you stock tips, it's time to get out of the market."

We were there through 2018 and 2019, and during the pandemic, it ran completely out of control, with every twenty-year-old out there buying GameStop and AMC on their phone with their stimulus money. It's irrational exuberance like we've never seen before, and the industry insiders know it.

WHEN IN DOUBT, STAY OUT

Warren Buffett and Charlie Munger of Berkshire Hathaway, two of the most renowned investors of modern times, have $149 billion in cash right now, more than 20 percent of their entire portfolio. It's the highest cash position they've ever had.

As I write near the start of 2022, the greatest investors of our generation don't trust current stock valuations. They want to be liquid to be able to take advantage of an illiquid market should we get there in the near future. They can't find value in the everything bubble since their model is to be patient, never chase, and let value work its magic over time.

The wealthiest investors are biding their time, waiting for a crash or steep pullback in equities, while the poorest people are sitting in the john at Burger King on their night shift, on the phone buying meme stocks, trying to get rich without putting in any effort. The instant gratification generation is now in the stock and crypto markets.

Buffett's famous quote is to "be fearful when others are greedy, and greedy when others are fearful." And right now, there is more greed than ever before. Everyone is bullish.

Sometimes the best move is patience. Sometimes the best trade is sitting on cash.

One of the best-kept secrets in the industry is that *cash is a position*; cash is choices, cash equals *options*, and you can do *anything* at *any time* if you have the cash to do it. Once you're *invested*, you no longer have those choices. If the market pulls back, that cash allows you to take full advantage and come out of the downturn ahead of the pack, buying cheap assets when others are panic-selling the stock they overpaid for months earlier.

I'm going to show you how to think more like the insiders. How to use the rules and a little bit of capital to pick off chances that don't drag you into the rest of the pool. How to react to what's happening, make your trade, and get out.

An educated speculator is like a surgeon who walks into the OR moments before the surgery, gets debriefed, gowns up, washes up, makes an incision, finishes the job, then stoically walks away while everyone else is still milling around in the theater. An educated speculator is surgical in their movement. As precise as a jet pilot.

In the hedge fund industry, they call it "head shots only." A sniper sitting up on a knoll doesn't just start firing and give away their position. You wait until you're absolutely sure you have the shot. You wait all day, all year if you have to, before the target gets into your crosshair, and then you pull the trigger. There are no second shots in sniper school. "One shot, one kill," as the saying goes. You wait until you are 100 percent certain.

You don't get emotionally attached. You don't romanticize anything.

You're not trying to convince anyone of anything, including yourself.

That was the biggest realization for me. I'd spent over a decade suffering from drug addiction and depression. I'd gone from being a punk kid who was fascinated by the markets to putting my name on four notable public companies and helping drive the growth of the new, legal cannabis industry. I'd gone from the bottom of the pond to the very top, but I learned that the sweet spot where I was happiest and where I ended up was somewhere in the middle.

Stealth is wealth, I learned. Time is too precious. If you want to soar with the eagles, you can't cluck around with the chickens.

I was reborn when I was twenty-nine years old. I suffered a couple motorcycle accidents, followed by some psychedelic therapy and "deep dives," in which I experienced a total ego death, watching myself lying on a gurney with my family around me saying goodbye. I realized that day (thanks to some 3-MMC and 5-MeO-DMT) that life is unfathomably valuable, precious, fragile, and brief. That every single breath is an absolute gift. That anything other than being present is a waste of time and energy.

You have a choice every morning to wake up heavy and depressed or wake up whistling and charged for what lies ahead. You can choose to add positivity to every room you're in. You can go to work to make someone else rich, or you can start to begin your own life's journey.

You can choose whatever you want. That's what makes the human experience so special.

The universe smacked me over the head. What I found with my second chance is that a regular, boring life is precious enough without the flash and pizazz if you can find fulfillment in what's real.

That's why I wrote down rules for myself in 2010, as a reminder of how to keep things in perspective, to keep myself under control, and to keep speculating for satisfaction, not simply for money. That's why I've decided to share them, because I believe that everyone should have the chance to become a completely free and autonomous individual.

We're not getting straight into the rules, however. Unlike most books about the markets, we're not going to start with business or money. Instead we're going to start with *you*. The first step to diving into your new life is to understand yourself. So let's go.

PART 1

YOUR MIND

What Do You Want to Be?

LOOK AROUND YOU

It's been said that you earn the average income of the ten people with whom you spend most time. How accurate that is, I don't know, but I have noticed that whenever I ask my wealthy friends about their finances—what they do about their taxes, how they treat their family trust, or how they manage cash flow—my financial picture for the coming quarters somehow seems to improve.

It's called osmosis.

Money is a type of energy. Hanging out with wealthy-minded people brings you more of that energy, and hanging out with people who have a poor mindset takes that energy away.

I always found it quite easy to adapt to whoever I was with, but I never quite belonged to any particular group, thanks partly to my ingrained distrust of other people. That started as a young child. I was soft-spoken and overly sensitive, but I was also compulsive and risk-seeking, so I hung out with the bad kids because I was different from the "normal" ones. I flipped from end to end of the spectrum and didn't feel at home anywhere.

I was always trying to figure out what I wanted to be when I grew up but also who I was in the first place.

I didn't let anyone get too close because I didn't trust them. I had a paranoid view of the world. I stopped sharing any personal information about myself.

The feeling of being written off made me reckless. I had no guideposts, especially after my dad died and there wasn't anyone I wanted to impress anymore, or anyone I was afraid of. Hanging out with really broken people made me feel better about myself.

As I grew up, my distrust spread to employers. I saw a job as meaning only that you were laying yourself open to being fired at any time. I felt like I couldn't rely on other people because, eventually, they all let you down.

ROLE MODELS

The market gives anyone the chance to be whoever they want to be. That's the independence it offers. But before you go into it, think about who *you* want to be. What sort of investor or trader will you be? You can be whoever you want, but one thing's for sure. If you're reckless, you'll get burned. There's no quicker way to lose your investment account than by trying to be someone you're not in the markets.

The Stock Market Is a Racket

A lot of rookies come into the market with a warped view of business that they probably got from watching *Wall Street* or *Boiler Room* or virtually any stock market movie. They think Jim Cramer from *Mad Money* on CNBC is what a stock trader looks like, with his rolled up sleeves and suspenders. For me, Cramer is everything that's wrong with the stock trading game, yelling at the camera like he's on a Wall Street trading floor, making out that he can see into the future because he used to manage a fund.

Cramer deals out his tips like they're some kind of sensational insights, but they're nothing special. The fact is, the belief on Wall Street has always been that he's no more than a wired shill for whatever corporation is paying him that month. Bought and paid for. Just like all the other bankers, brokers, analysts, fund managers, and other talking heads. They all collect a paycheck from a firm, and that firm will cut anyone and anything down for quarterly profits.

You don't have to listen to Cramer. And you shouldn't. Cramer's job is to drag unsuspecting rookies into a world of frenetic trading, where they're always trying to leap on the next big thing—and are always just missing it. Chasing tips never works out long term.

Before anyone starts trading stock, they have to understand this: like a casino or a horse track, the stock market exists to try to take your money from you. It is a giant wealth transfer tool. Cramer is part of the racket. He wants you to jump right in because he knows you'll likely lose your money . . . and new money—*your* money—is what fuels the market. You are liquidity, and a million yous is what any given fund needs to offload their giant positions as the masses pile into it; the stock market is called the "secondary market" for a reason. Retail comes in as institutions exit positions and go back to cash to fund other startups that you'll be buying two to three years after them in the *secondary market*.

Don't jump in blind. If you're new to stock trading, that's the most important lesson to learn. Until you've figured out why you're getting into the markets, what you want to achieve, and how you are going to achieve it, you're unlikely to survive. You're cannon fodder for the pros.

Every New Investor and Trader Needs Guidance

I had no role models for becoming a normal adult, let alone becoming a stock trader. I didn't know anyone who knew anything about behavioral economics—why we do what we do with money—so when I started to trade, I read a lot of books. The most powerful were two of the oldest: *Think and Grow Rich* by Napoleon Hill was published back in 1937; *The Power of Positive Thinking* by Norman Vincent Peale came out in 1952. Their age didn't matter. They both contained profound truths about our relationship with money.

What Hill and Peale showed me—and Ryan Holiday in a more recent book, *The Obstacle Is the Way* (2014)—is that, although there's a reason people stay in jobs they hate, they really don't have to, and they shouldn't. There are people who generate millions in income for themselves without needing a traditional job or career, simply by learning to understand their relationship with money, by changing their employment (slave) mindset, and by putting their money to work, be it in business, equities, or crypto.

They opt out of modern slavery and become *The Sovereign Individual* (1997), which is a phenomenally in-depth book on the topic by James Dale Davidson.

Anyone can step off the nine-to-five treadmill.

Those books are still essential reading for every trader. I'd recommend everyone read them and many, many more before they place a single dollar on a trade. Understand who you are up against and who is behind the curtain. Get yourself to a place of deep understanding of the mechanics of trading and how Wall Street works. *Reminiscences of a Stock Operator* (1923) by Edwin Lefèvre is great insight into Wall Street mechanics and the mind of a trader. It applies even more today than it did in 1923.

Read the Fucking Manual

My dad was always horrible with money. I could have used that as a crutch to follow him into a life of financial struggle. Instead I looked at his example, looked at what I had, and thought, "Well, I have a healthy relationship with money, and I'm not going to jeopardize that." Instead of learning how to fix his money problems, he just went on his entire life without reading any of the money manuals and wondered why he didn't know how it worked.

So I started to read and I kept on reading. I've read more than a hundred books about markets and behavioral economics. I've spent more than twenty thousand hours analyzing stock charts. I've taught myself to become a professional investor. But the most important lesson I learned was this: don't trade before you know what you're doing. Do the work. RTFM: read the fucking manual. Paper-trade first.

That's the least you can do if you want a career or even a part-time vocation in the stock market: treat it like a business.

If you're going to be a technical trader, then get yourself the right technical education and tools. I have used everything from Trade Navigator to TradingView and often find myself reverting back to the web-based options to keep things simple and accessible across all devices. Less is more when it comes to technical software, because there are tools to allow you to work from anywhere, quickly and without cumbersome localized software on your machines. The web now has every technical indicator you could ever need, for free. Yes, it might be delayed by fifteen minutes, but you can pay small fees to get real-time data for most exchanges. Investopedia. com is always there to answer any questions you will have in the beginning. I also pay about fifty dollars per month on StockCharts. com for real-time feed, and there is nothing I can't do on there right in my web browser.

Nothing Is Instant

When people come to my home and ask me how I managed to become a full-time investor, I point to the bookshelves and say, "It's all there. Grab that book by Napoleon Hill and read it." They rarely do. It's too much effort. They just want the Coles Notes. They want you to tell them the secret.

They want to make a living by speculating, but they're not prepared to read even a single book or dedicate a month or two to becoming technically proficient with the mechanics of trading stock.

It's human behavior to want instant gratification, but it's completely unrealistic in the money game. These are the same people who ask me everyday something like, "Should I buy ABC Co at thirty-five bucks?" I tell them, "I'd wait until it's twenty-five bucks." A week later, I get a text saying, "How did you know it was going to come back to twenty-five?"

The answer is I didn't know; I made an educated guess. I looked at the stock's chart. I figured out its technical patterns, recognized an unsustainable move upward and, because I've spent so long looking at stock charts—the equivalent of almost eight hundred working weeks—I got a good indication of where it was headed in the near term. Or at least, I could see that it has more than a 90 percent probability of seeing 25 before it sees 45 for various micro and macro reasons.

It happens every day. And it's not that I'm special in any way; I've just put in the work to be able to look at the chart and say, "Well, it's far more likely to do this than that—here's why." That only comes with seeing it thousands and thousands of times. I did what a handicapper does at the ponies. I saw that it was a nine-to-one odds that the stock would drop before it went higher, based on three obvious factors. I tell them, "Well, the RSI is deeply overbought, the volume is petering out, and it's just about to fall below its fifty-day moving average after five big green days in a row. It's going to pull back and fill the gap."

They say, "Oh wow. I don't even know what any of that means."

And I tell them, "Stop. Trading. Stock. Start learning."

If there's one thing the market loves more than idiots with money, it's lazy idiots with money.

When a rookie trader loses all their money, they turn around and blame the system. It's not the system. They just didn't take it seriously enough. They didn't RTFM.

This Is Not a Video Game

The system is rigged against independent traders. It's set up to seem as harmless as possible, but it's deadly dangerous. Think about trading stock as gambling. That's exactly what it is; it just calls itself something different.

In the past, Las Vegas used to call itself the center of the *gambling* industry. Now it's referred to as the *gaming* industry. In the late 1990s, Nevada governor Brian Sandoval came up with the new name, which is subtly but profoundly different. If you walk into a *gambling* environment, you're immediately on your guard and feeling vulnerable; if you walk into a *gaming* establishment, you're ready to be entertained. It sounds not only less dangerous but downright enjoyable.

Las Vegas repackaged gambling as gaming so that more people would come and lose their money, willingly, and have fun doing it.

The stock market has been gamified in the same way as Las Vegas. Too many people treat trading like a game, which can have devastating consequences. Stocks are what pension funds put their money into. They're the heart of the free market economy. They represent real equity in a real company, and the commission you pay to trade on a stock exchange is your money. Buying shares is like buying into a real estate contract. It has implications.

Beware of the Gateway

I know a lot about the stock market, and I know a lot about cannabis. From 2008 onward, I blended the two together as a vocation, as I was helplessly addicted to both and saw the marriage between them as a perfect union to validate my two loves. Both can negatively impact your life if you let them.

Cannabis was my early gateway drug and window into altered states. I smoked a lot of pot from a young age and then did a lot of recreational psychedelics—and continue to do so—and they're the best things I have ever done as far as personal growth is concerned. I felt that I might as well try everything at least twice—but I was lucky enough to get away with it; most do not. For a lot of people coming up nowadays, penny stocks are the gateway drug to a serious addiction. They start trading cheap stocks and then bigger names, then they think, "I might as well sell short-term options on margin."

Not many people can get away with that sort of logic. Just because you've traded some equities does not make you an expert in the whole market—quite the opposite.

There are no warning labels on gambling machines or playing cards. Or on stocks, options, cryptocurrencies, or NFTs.

LOOK OUT FOR THE SCAM

The stock market is a manic place. It is *mania most of the time*. When the movie *Wolf of Wall Street* came out in 2013, I was pleased because it showed everyone how many people in the stock market are totally disconnected from reality in their world of drugs, Lambos, and hookers. And the movie wasn't even an extreme version of the truth. To me, the words "investment banker" or "stock broker" typically suggest someone who is compulsive and an extremist.

In other words, someone like me.

These guys are super professional in the boardroom in their Armani suits, but by 2:00 a.m. they're in strip clubs blowing thousands hanging out with the girls. The job attracts a type of compulsive, addictive personality because they have to be able to carve a living out of a zero-sum game. They can only buy their suits and drugs and girls on the backs of other people's hard work. That's what a capital markets broker, or "investment advisor," does. He leverages other people's money. Your fees are his party favors. Without your money, he has no income.

My money and your money.

The people who appear to want to make money for you—from crazy Jim Cramer to the stock market "investment advisor" who calls you up to give you an inside tip from the iBanker who's putting a bunch of capital into a NewCo—are all really just trying to take your wealth away. To separate you and your capital. To turn your nest egg into an order. Into liquidity for those in before you. Into fees payable to them and the firm.

Like drug dealers on the street or blackjack dealers in the casino, their *only* job is to get you to give them your money. That's it. The rest is all a distraction to lure you in.

You're on the outside, and those guys are on the inside, so they have an obvious and immediate advantage. They're better at it than you are because it's their job, while you might be going in vastly underprepared or, worse, not taking it as seriously as you should.

Let's say Mr. Smith goes to a stockbroker to open an account because he wants to start trading. He hands over his money, and the broker starts placing orders for him. Mr. Broker is going to make a hundred bucks every time he enters or exits a stock for Mr. Smith. Whether that stock goes up or down matters a lot for Mr. Smith, but it means nothing from an actual risk perspective to Mr. Broker because he's paid regardless if Mr. Smith wins or loses, like the casino dealer.

If Mr. Smith decides not to buy anything, the broker doesn't generate any income off him that day. So often, the broker tries to persuade him to make trades and initiate new positions due to the hot tip of the day from Mr. Analyst upstairs. Mr. Smith wants to wait, but the broker drops a little FOMO sentence or two. The stock drops after his buy, and Mr. Smith complains to his wife, "I should have waited." The broker doesn't care because he's off spending Mr. Smith's money on martinis with the boys after the market closes.

Ask yourself this. If this guy or gal knew anything about anything, why wouldn't they trade their own money as their vocation? Why would they work for nothing but commission? And why on earth would anyone put their trust in a guy who's not even putting in his own money but just using yours? Yes, like the police, many brokers are good people trying to do a good job, but the system is fundamentally broken, serving only those who are within it.

The broker business is systematically predatory and inherently flawed.

I've been opposed to brokers working on commission my entire life. It's an outright conflict of interest. It makes their job simply to persuade people to make trades, not to guide them toward good trades and away from the bad. Nothing at all about money management.

Just like learning nothing relevant to life through four wasted years of high school or up to eight years in college.

When it's investment banking, it's the same. It's just that the sums and accounts are larger. The banker has no skin in the game. The banker rarely ever cuts a check. And when they do cut what's called a "pro" check into the deal, it's almost never more than the actual commission they are paid on the deal. In other words it cost them zero dollars, yet they love to tout it like it's coming right out of their savings. It's not. It's another black spot in the business.

This is part of the reason people hate bankers and stockbrokers. They often portray an "in it together" mentality while they are an agent of a company trained to separate you from your capital. Trained to give the hard sell, manage rebuttals, and keep all the risk on your back, not theirs. They hold Presidents Clubs annually, where they gather and tell stories about clients while the firm hands out big awards for those who generated the most commission that year.

It's no different from when you walk into a casino. The blackjack dealer looking at you is a professional with probably sixteen decks in his shoe. Statistically, that makes him twenty-two times more likely to beat you time and again. If you do manage to beat him once or twice, he just needs to keep you playing. Eventually, he will win.

His only job the whole day is to get money out of you. And you'd better believe that he's good at it.

Keep Them Trading

Las Vegas learned long ago that the biggest trick is to keep the punters in the casino. As long as the punters are in there, they keep gambling. They'll get tired, they'll get more reckless, and they will lose.

There's a scene in the movie *Casino* where a wealthy Chinese gambler flies in and has a hot streak for a week. He's about to leave with a million dollars, but the casino tells him there's a problem with the plane he was about to depart on, and they give him a suite for the extra night—and that night he loses all the money.

That's how the casinos use psychology to keep you gambling. They give you a suite, they boost your credit, and they give you a seat at the blackjack table with the high rollers.

Stockbroking is the same. Keep them bidding, keep them trading, keep them high.

The book *The Psychology of Money* (2020) by Morgan Housel is a tremendous primer on how psychology influences all markets from the casino to the stock exchanges and everywhere in between. Any books that you can get your hands on about human behavioral economics will dramatically help increase your odds of winning while gambling.

If you don't start looking out for the psychology of the situation, eventually you'll start to lose and not know why. And once you lose, you'll lose more because you keep trying to get back to even, unable to find the culprit because you aren't aware of the psychology taking place.

But you don't have to be a part of it at all. The system might be rigged, but if you know the rules, you can start shifting the odds back in your favor.

That's what distinguishes a successful speculator from someone who wins big and blows it all—or who loses big and never trades again.

Everyone's At It

If the stock market sounds like the Wild West, it's because it is. Even large, respected financial institutions are often careless with money—yours and mine, not their own—and sometimes downright corrupt. And they get away with it. The bigger the scam, the more involved the big banks and brokerage firms are. It's easier for them to hide that way and claim they didn't find the red flags in their due diligence. We've now got financial crime fines upward of a billion dollars handed out to some of the biggest financial institutions in the world.

No one bats an eye. Almost no one does any prison time.

Michael Milken of Drexel Burnham Lambert wrote the manual on how to rip people off in the 1980s when he got the investment bank into insider dealing in the junk bond market, which sold high-yield, high-risk bonds that the regular markets won't touch. The bank made a billion dollars profit in a single year from funding huge corporate mergers and acquisitions—pumping and dumping —before it was eventually forced into bankruptcy. Milken went to jail, but his colleagues didn't get punished at all.

The book *Billion Dollar Whale* (2018) tells a true story from the 2010s of a Malaysian named Jho Low, who tricked Goldman Sachs into helping him swindle $5 billion from a Malaysian sovereign wealth fund over a whole decade. Goldman Sachs only had to carry out due diligence on the one guy, and they couldn't even get that right. They enabled the entire fraud.

Right after the scam was discovered, Jho Low disappeared. To this day, no one knows where he is. But we do know where some of his money went. He funded the movie *Wolf of Wall Street*, which is ironic as all hell. A movie about corruption on Wall Street was funded by the proceeds of financial crime because the world's biggest, most prestigious, and notorious investment bank helped make it all a reality.

Even today, Goldman is in the business of selling derivatives out the front door while betting against them round the back. Meanwhile, Big Pharma is raising a generation of kids on amphetamines, antianxiety, and antidepressant drugs. In the United States, 80 percent of all heroin addicts started out with a doctor's prescription for opioids. Big Pharma paid clinics to dish out opioids, and when people couldn't get their scripts filled by a pharmacist, they ended up on the street buying heroin. The doctors started the opiate epidemic.

The very businesses that are supposed to be protecting the customer are the ones that are throwing them to the wolves.

JP Morgan recently paid a billion-dollar fine for manipulating the silver market on the COMEX in Chicago. They see it as the cost of doing business. In the casino business, it's a form of leakage. If you rip off ten customers and the eleventh guy takes a little bit of money out of the building, that's leakage—and it's absolutely fine. As long as the first ten gave you their cash already, everyone's happy, and the scam keeps going.

It's Tilted against You

Finance can be an ugly world. The chances of a brand-new independent investor stepping into the markets and coming out alive are slim to none. And if you try it with no education, no training, and no guidelines, you're definitely not going to survive.

The system is tilted against the little guy.

When you buy a stock on the stock market, especially a junior penny stock or a startup tech company, promoters are already pushing that stock and likely exiting their cheap or free positions onto you. The investment bankers have owned the paper since the start, made their money, and are eager to get out. So by the time you get the email that announces, "The next 300 percent biotech stock has arrived. Click here," it's got nothing to do with whether the business is sound or not, and everything to do with shifting the stock from their hands into yours.

It's a scam.

It's daylight robbery. A smash-and-grab by bros in gold cufflinks.

NO PLACE FOR FOOLS

Whenever buying a stock makes you feel smart, think again. If somebody sold it to you in any way at all, it might already be overvalued.

You've just become what the market calls "the greater fool." The person buying something only because he thinks there are other people that are going to pay him more for it later. He needs a greater fool to take it off his hands for more money in order to "win."

Unless you intend to be a long-term investor because you really love a company, once you buy a stock, you need to find someone willing to pay more than you paid for the exact same thing. The whole stock market is based on the premise that whatever someone pays for a stock today, there will be an investor (or an idiot) willing to pay more tomorrow.

Know this and try to never forget it. This is an important key to the game.

Everyone is looking for the greater fool to pass their stock on in this huge game of hot potato: swashbucklers, brokers, bankers, businesses, gamblers, liars, and thieves.

It's financial warfare, exchanging paper like gunfire, all dressed up as a profession.

Expect to spend most of your time in a foxhole taking fire. And make sure your position is as strong as possible. Make sure your mag is full, make sure you have an escape plan, and for god's sake, make sure you remain calm and keep your eyes peeled.

The kind of stock trader you are depends entirely upon what you want to be. The choice is up to you.

I wish someone had explained that to me when I was younger. I wish I didn't have to find out for myself how important it is to think carefully about who you spend time with. About *osmosis*. About how you can take twenty dollars to a crack den and within minutes be smoking crack, or you can go to the office of the local Chamber of Commerce and become a member of the business community. About the consequences of quitting high school before graduation; if you don't graduate high school, your chances of ending up dead or in jail rise dramatically. Your chances of ever becoming a six-figure earner fall to less than one in ten.

It's the same thing in the stock market. If you don't give your-self a tremendous education—reading books, tracking stocks, and getting a really good lay of the land—you're going to end up dead in the water. The odds against you will be the same as the odds against the high school dropout.

You'll be chewed up and spit out and working the night shift at the Pita Pit in no time.

When it comes to trading in the markets for the first time, everyone is a high school dropout. You have no knowledge and no experience. The odds are massively tilted against you. It's like sitting at a poker table with a bunch of professional gamblers. You might look like the other players, but you don't have to be a mathematician to figure out that the odds are deeply stacked against you. And yet many rookie stock traders kid themselves, "I've got a good chance here."

They really don't. They don't even realize that they're sitting at the same table as the professionals. Even if they get lucky once or twice, they're not going to have the knowledge to know when to walk away. They'll keep betting, and eventually the numbers say they'll lose.

The market *needs* them to lose so that the professionals can win—just like the stock and crypto markets.

Educate Yourself

The very thing I love about being an *independent investor*, which is that I can trade from home with no one else involved, is what makes it so dangerous. At the other end of every click are traders, or even trading algorithms, trying to take my money.

Again, opening your screen and starting to trade is like sitting down with professional poker players and expecting to win. It's an irrational expectation that's based more on greed than reality if you're not at their level.

Rookies sometimes wonder why they lose and lose and lose when they start trading stock. The answer is simple. They're up against me, who has twenty thousand hours of experience and understands how to fade in and out of a forming trend like a ghost, carving out double-digit gains before most retailers are aware of the action taking place. Momentum is an energy that you are either tapped into or you're not. If you're not feeling which way the price is going, get out; you need that conviction, which comes from believing you are equipped and informed. That confidence serves as race fuel.

No one should trade until they know the basics, just like no one should go to the casino to play blackjack or poker until they've learned the math.

It's all about constantly educating yourself. Being independent doesn't mean you can get away without understanding the market. If you're attracted to stock trading because you think it's less work than a regular job, you're wrong. It's not a lazy option. You can't have your cake and eat it too. If you want the product, you have to put in the effort.

You should aim to be advancing every day, educating yourself as if your survival depends on it.

The market can smell a lack of experience. It chews up new-comers. Sometimes when people bemoan their bad luck or are genuinely puzzled at how they lost their cash, I point out the global risks or the technical indicators that should have warned them against this or that trade.

You'd be amazed at how many of them say they'd never even heard of any sort of due diligence tools. You're simply fooling yourself if you think you can play in these pools and survive against experts without the proper skillset.

Getting Technical

I got chewed up a lot in my first five years in the markets. In hindsight, I was trading blindfolded. Every month when I was trying to figure out my lousy results, I got a little more knowledge. I learned how important volume and momentum are. I focused on technical courses and learned all that I could about charting, seasonality, and technical indicators. Every piece of information made me a little less likely to be eaten by the market.

Everyone can access the exact same data the professionals have; the key is learning how to interpret it in the same way a specialist doctor can look at charts or MRIs in a quantitative way to figure out the best treatment for a patient. That's all a professional stock trader does. They look at the indicators and come up with the most likely outcome. Same with horse race handicappers and professional poker players.

Most rookie traders don't want to take the time even to learn about technical indicators or macroeconomic trends, let alone human behavior. The technical indicators are microeconomics;

macroeconomics are the broader top-down picture, such as: Is the government going to introduce a new tax plan? Will that affect the technology sector and therefore tech stocks? Is it going to be a wet spring? Should I scale out of Sun Tan Inc. and buy shares in Umbrella Corp?

While I was learning the ropes, I lost money every day, every week, and every year for five years straight. I thought I didn't have to follow the rules, because that was what I was used to in the rest of my life. I went after instant gratification and failed to put in the prerequisite time.

That lasted until I got my ass handed to me. That's when I decided to stop being lazy and follow the rules. And it was only then that I started making my $300-per-day target. And that the target eventually started to march upward.

BE A HUMBLE STUDENT

You have to become a student of the market. I'm still learning how it works and all its little nuances every day, and what continues to astound me is how little I knew back when I started my trading journey. I thought I was a guru, but I knew *nothing* in the grand scheme of things. And ten or fifteen years from now, I'll probably feel the same way about myself today.

That kind of humble student outlook is imperative to have longevity in the trading game.

Look at the example set by Warren Buffett, one of the greatest investors of our lifetime. Buffett reads fifteen newspapers every morning because he believes an investor can't get enough news and data. Aged ninety-one, he's still a sponge for data that might influence the market.

Accept Nothing as the Truth and Everything as a Possibility

I started taking my positions based on the grounds that I know nothing until I do. I would be as defensive as I could. I was going to take the mentality that if I could make $300 a day, that was enough. I knew that $400 billion changes hands on Wall Street every twenty-four hours, another $20 billion in Canada. So if I can take three hundred bucks out of that, if I can take my little crumb, I'm good, because that helps me individually to become more valuable to the economy as I help drive interest in many areas, generating a lot of tax karma as well as jobs and professional fees for our friends in suits.

It's a mentality shift. I quit thinking, "Oh man, I missed that trade. I could have made so much more." I learned to take my money and be grateful. It's like going out to sea to catch your fish for the day. You don't need to fill the boat because you can go back out tomorrow. Focus on today's goals, and trust that the weeks, months, and quarters will seemingly start to take care of themselves.

Set the target for what you need rather than what you think might be available. And set it according to where you are and what your bite size is.

Everyone has a bite size that they're accustomed to. When I first set out, cutting a $5,000 check made my stomach churn. Now it's $250,000 before I get any butterflies. You don't jump straight into big trades when you're a newcomer. You work your way up accordingly.

Learn about Asset Allocation before You Start to Deploy or Purchase Assets

Asset allocation is how you know when you're winning and why—and how you can easily survive when you're losing.

Happiness and success is all about knowing the level you are at and the level you need to be at.

Many independent capital market investors don't know anyone involved in the financial industry, nor did I when I started my own journey. But you can find mentorship anywhere.

You can hop on YouTube and search "technical analysis," which will yield you everything you could ever need and a whole lot more. Grab your laptop and headphones, and you can start to educate yourself for nothing by watching videos about the basic 101 you need to know on conducting technical analysis. How to spot a breakout. How to lock in gains. How to protect yourself using stop-losses or dollar cost averaging over time to take advantage of price fluctuations.

There's no reason not knowing anyone who is in the markets needs to stop you. It's no excuse even though you've been using it all this time. And if you do come across someone who's involved, and who you admire, pick their brain. Ask them questions. Ask if you can do some work with them for free in return for a chance to learn.

Where do you do your trading? What tools do you find most helpful? What type of instruments do you like to trade? What do you look for? Anything you really like right now, and why? Those are the types of things to ask, because with every little crumb of information you gather, you start to put things together to create a meal. Not to mention that the recipient of the question will feel a sort of obligation to explain why, since your questions are valid, and he himself needs to be able to explain them if he is a sound investor. You could almost use the mindset of learning this investing trade by pretending you are mentoring someone else; you are always describing everything in detail in order to assure yourself as much as to ensure you always maintain a student outlook in your journey to ten thousand hours of technical analysis.

All the information is out there; much of it is free. You just have to learn how to look for it.

If you want to find it enough, you can: you just have to put in the work. So the question is, will you? The answer comes down to a couple of questions. Are you happy with your current financial situation? And if you're not, do you have an income shortfall problem, or do you have a spending rate problem? That's how you start to work out whether stock trading is for you. Who do you want to be, and how can money help you get there? You need to know the *why* before any other details will matter.

Money Isn't Everything

Anyone can make money. In today's world, it's not that difficult to make a million dollars. What's difficult is keeping it or growing it. Having that million a year later is nearing on impossible. And turning it into two million defies the laws of gravity—without the right mindset. As soon as someone thinks, "I've made it," they stop the hustle but continue to spend. They immediately start walking backward.

Mike Tyson made $500 million in six or seven years in the ring. By the tenth year, he had zero dollars. He was bankrupt. Most wealthy people have declared bankruptcy, many of them more than once. Everyone is also now aware of the lottery phenomenon: the ability of a financial windfall to completely wipe someone out financially, sometimes in an impressively short period of time.

UNDERSTAND YOUR MONEY

Money is difficult to hold on to if you've been programmed to believe that it's hard to get. It's been said that if you took all the world's wealth and distributed every single dollar evenly to the 7.9 billion inhabitants on the planet, within two years, things would go right back to the way they were before.

That's because money has its own way of flowing.

Wealth Comes with Problems

I've been poor and depressed, and I've been wealthy and depressed. I don't recommend either. In many ways, I was happiest when I was making my $300 per day, which was enough to live modestly, but not enough to bring any money problems.

Because wealth doesn't come without problems. When I first made some money, I felt like I'd reached the top of the mountain, and then I found out that there was nothing up there. It was cold and barren, and I didn't have a coat. Not only that. Suddenly, I had a bunch of problems that I didn't know existed. Now I needed to be more insured. I needed good corporate and legal help. I needed better accounting and full-time bookkeeping. I needed to have a much deeper relationship with the taxman.

I needed to protect my moneymaking system from negligence and from myself.

My wealth took away some of my freedom in the early days and became a burden. It's the lottery phenomenon: the windfall that overwhelms people and makes them miserable.

And it's real. To avoid it, you have to deepen your understanding of the flow of money.

Level Up and Grow with Your Money

When I first had some money, my mind wasn't ready for it. In my head, I was still poor. I had a poverty mindset that didn't give myself permission to enjoy any wealth. I didn't think I deserved it. That crippled me and stifled my growth. It was like I was trying to keep myself small by worrying incessantly and manifesting new issues that I could have avoided.

My friends were patting me on the back and celebrating my success, and I would look at them with confusion. A little money accumulation made me feel horrible inside now that they all saw me as "successful"—therefore implying they were "less successful." I didn't like that feeling at all. I was more stressed than I had ever been; I was an alien again.

You have to grow with your money. Ladder up, because nothing will screw someone up more than just dumping a bunch of money in their lap.

Recognize when You're Wealthy

The only difference between a rich man and a poor man is that the poor man spends more than he makes.

In other words, wealth is a mentality. If you have enough to live as you want to live, you're rich. If you make $500 million like Mike Tyson, and you go insolvent because you buy tigers and give your friends jets, then you're poor.

It doesn't matter how much material wealth you accumulate. If you have a poor money brain, you're a fool with money. And as people have been saying since the days of ancient Rome, a fool and his money will soon be parted. Another variation on the theme is that if an idiot gets some money, just add time and it'll be gone.

It's all about your attitude toward money.

If you have a pair of shoes, a mattress, and one dollar, you're among the richest people on this planet. You just have to recognize it. Many of earth's inhabitants don't even have that.

Jeff Bezos has as many money problems as a single mom on welfare. It doesn't matter that the checks he writes have got six or seven zeros. He still has the same cash flow crunches and stressors and hundreds of personal staff to deal with directly on a weekly basis who manage tens of thousands of people below them.

Money doesn't solve every problem. People tell themselves, "If I just had five hundred grand in the bank, I wouldn't be so stressed."

It's horseshit.

Everyone thinks that way instead of acknowledging where they are: "I have a pair of shoes. I have a dollar in my wallet, and I'm not hungry. I'm already rich, period. I'm rich because I'm not hungry or cold."

That's the paradigm shift. You're not homeless; you're not starving. You're already rich! Now let's work on increasing your wealth.

INCREASING YOUR WEALTH

Once you acknowledge your richness in terms of health, time, freedom, as well as paper currency, you can go ahead and start to increase your *wealth*. You can start creating what I call a runway: enough money to cover you for at least a year or two without having to go back to the mill.

That's starting to build real wealth.

Don't Work for Your Money; Make Your Money Work for You

Around 2,400 years ago, the *Tao Te Ching*, the basic scripture of Taoism, said that if you become "successful" and hoard a giant pile of gold, you're going to spend the rest of your life identifying with it, polishing it, protecting it, insuring it, talking about it, and staring at it. You won't even be able to leave your house because you're afraid someone will try to take it in your absence.

So you now work for your gold. You give up your freedom to be "rich."

The ancient scripture paints a vivid picture of what is as much a disease of the mind as being poor-minded is on the other side of it.

It's a real trap to watch out for. When I was fifteen, I knew drug dealers that wouldn't leave the house. They had a little safe holding their cash, and they couldn't leave home because someone might try to rob them. Today, I know stock jockeys worth $500 million who won't do anything but watch their portfolio from market open to market close each and every day. They're afraid to look away or take a break in case something happens while they're not at their screens.

That's what I call Scrooge McDuck syndrome.

You need to stay on top of your money. If you're lying awake at night wondering about what type of life insurance you should be buying, you've let money get on top of you.

Money Flees a Poor Environment

Most people's primary problem when it comes to their finances isn't money; it's mindset. You have to have the right mentality because money will flee an inhospitable environment. That's just what it does. If you win the lottery and spend it all on houses and cars, then pretty soon, you'll be mortgaging the houses and selling the cars to pay the bills as life gets more and more expensive. You're not going to have any money left because you completely failed to realize that for every dollar out, you should have one or more coming in if you want to maintain that quality of life.

If anyone gets some cash, the first thing they ask themselves is, "What do I do with it?" More often than not, the only smart answer is nothing. Leave it alone. But that's not how the human brain works. It wants to *do*, not just *be*. When it comes to money, our instinct is not to sit idly by. It is to invest, to spend, to churn and burn—to transact. But money is just energy, and you're going to burn through it and mishandle or fumble that energy.

Kirk Kerkorian was the child of Armenian immigrants. His dad struggled, his mom, like mine, put the kids in used clothes, and the family moved from home to home. His parents treated money as something elusive they weren't entitled to enjoy. They weren't on this earth to be rich. They came here with a "lacking mindset," a tendency to think that money is elusive and hard to find. Kerkorian decided as a kid, "I will never be like my parents." He dedicated his life to not being a poor thinker. He became a professional gambler and eventually a billionaire and a very important philanthropist. *The Gambler: How Penniless Dropout Kirk Kerkorian Became the Greatest Deal Maker in Capitalist History* is a 2018 biography written by William C. Rempel that I highly recommend for anyone interested in American business history. Kerkorian shaped Las Vegas, had a significant influence in Hollywood, and was a titan in the automotive industry.

If he had been brought up in a comfortable home and didn't bother to teach himself about the rules of money, he would have had a much smaller impact on the world.

Wage Earning Is a Hamster Wheel

The Industrial Revolution changed our relationship with wealth when it made clocks the authority and created the mentality of punching in and out: *serving time.* That's the wage-earner mindset: we enjoy our allocated two-week annual vacation, but in the meantime, we'll put in our hours and sit in the pub and moan after hours about our managers.

Most of the world lives like that. Many apparently wealthy people are slaves to earning wages. The entrepreneur Gary Vaynerchuk points out that someone can have a Ferrari, a huge home, and a Rolex or two, but if they have no money in the bank, they're a slave to the very things they've bought to try to look wealthy. Worse still, they now need twenty-five grand a month just to maintain the facade.

That's not freedom. That's called being house-poor or living way beyond your means.

It's not worth creating an appearance of success if it traps you on a hamster wheel. You'll burn through your money just trying to keep up with the Joneses since there will always be people who are "further ahead"—whatever that means.

A wage-earning job takes eight or more hours a day in exchange for enough money so that you can go home, sleep, repeat, and show up again in the morning. Working to live has ultimately become living to work. Wage earners are the living dead: matrix zombies living exclusively off matrix food delivered to them, endless streaming content, booze, and porn. It's worse than a hamster wheel. At least the hamster gets to stretch his legs and drink clean water.

Half the workforce say they feel completely unfulfilled all over the world.

The other half are lying.

Wages Will Make You a Living, but Profits Will Make You a Fortune

A specialist doctor can make a tremendous living, but he will never have a fortune if he trades his time for money. Even the greatest expert only has so much time. A businessman or an industrialist makes profits, and that's how he creates a fortune. It might be a modest fortune, but he's wealthy, and he doesn't have a nine-to-five job, or even a six-to-nine job. He's not on the hamster wheel because he gets large quarterly profits flowing through to him as dividends, and he manages that cash flow effectively to ensure he's always thriving and never just surviving.

Money is fuel, like gasoline in your car. You only need a certain amount, and then, you fill up again. You don't worry about where your next tank is going to come from. Imagine getting in your car in Seattle to drive to Los Angeles. If we treated gas like we treat money, we'd load the trunk and back seats with jerricans and fill them all with gas "just in case." Then, whenever we found another gas station, we'd fill them all up again. We'd never have enough fuel on hand—in our mind, anyway.

Money is the same! Know this; understand this.

Everyone has just that mindset about money. There's never, ever enough. It's like sand falling through our fingers. Just when it comes in, it goes right back out.

But the reality is that there will be ample ways to get gasoline— or to make more money. Almost without exception.

Don't treat money as if it's sand between your fingers, or it'll always feel like it's flowing away from you. Treat it like fuel. It's the go juice for experiences. It's fun coupons for the paywalls of life.

And keep in mind that money wants and needs to flow, so hoarding and not giving or spending won't end well. The same goes for earning, and earning but spending three times as much as you earn: that won't end well either. Find the balance. The yin and yang to your cash flow. Let money flow freely, and get out of the way in terms of thinking that you "earned it" or "spent it." You're simply a temporary custodian, a counterpart for a buyer or a seller of any product or service. Be grateful to be in the wheel of commerce.

It's Easier to Make Money than Time

Money is the most abundant commodity on this planet. There are ten million different ways to make it. People tell you that money is elusive, but it is the easiest thing to get ahold of. You can go anywhere and sell papers, flip burgers, do many different "start today" jobs in almost any town on earth in exchange for local fiat currency. Can't pay rent? Wash dishes. Don't want to wash dishes? Sell something. Zoom out and get off the wheel of slavery and poverty because you *need* and you *can't* and you *won't*. Make the required changes today.

Making More Time Is Impossible

Time is finite. It's the one thing we can't make more of. And yet everybody has a completely inverse attitude that money is special and time is not. We willingly, daily, over decades, give up one for the other: the time for the money.

Folks, the reality is that you are doing it backward—180 degrees from freedom.

Realizing that the opposite was true was what brought my freedom.

I read years ago that the first step to achieving any meaningful financial independence is your resignation letter. Every time. It takes courage, yes—but all great things do. Only when you remove the safety net—the plan B—can you start to go out and bring value to this world by following through on plan A: creating a brand, a business, or a vocation that will create income to generate wealth, not just a stipend for the rent as you stare out the window thinking about all the shoulds and coulds. If you're billing out for something you're good at, you're time limited. But if you hire someone to replicate your work, you effectively make *more* time. Now you can create wealth even if you're not working. If you create an automated options trading system, you can earn money every day whether you look at your screen or not.

Mailbox money. It comes whether you're in the office, the bathtub, or the Caribbean.

ASSET ALLOCATION

I have "asset allocation" tattooed on my arm.

It's everything. It essentially means that your assets are balanced. Imagine your day, your most valuable of all assets, as a pie: you cut slices to make time for relationships, for colleagues, for work, for eating, for talking to your partner, for yourself. Now imagine your financial assets the same way. You carve out the pie in the way that gets the best results: some real estate, some cash, some savings, some investments, some play money.

Warren Buffett attributes his entire $100 billion net worth to one thing: asset allocation. He knows how to cut the pie.

Without asset allocation, someone who wins a million bucks on the lottery will be poor in three months. With good asset allocation, they can protect their million and potentially double it every few years.

Don't Be Like Cattle

Work provides wage earners with food and shelter, but it also puts them on a free-range tax farm. We're all wearing barcodes too: your social security number in the US and your social insurance number in Canada. If you think you're a free individual and not on a tax farm, try not filing your taxes.

You'll soon find out how free you really are.

It's almost impossible to be self-reliant anymore, ever since fiat, government-backed "cash" took over from bartering as the main means of economic exchange. We need to bring back self-reliance through agorism, but in the meantime, the stock market can offer independence to those willing to become eager students.

Money enables you to create a *runway*. Once you have twenty-four months of money put away and allocated properly, you're effectively financially independent—at least for the time being.

Can *you* do that?

The first goal is a twelve-month runway. You put some gas in the tank for six months, then you have six months left to make it happen. That's not to say that the rest of your life goes on hold while you're getting ready to trade. Don't obsess about money; do something you enjoy instead. You need enough of a runway before the plane can take flight.

Don't mix up money with the point of the exercise, which is independence. Money is just the gasoline. It's decision fuel. Travel juice. Before you go on a road trip in your car, the last thing you're thinking about is if there will be enough gas in your future.

You can always get more.

Money Is Energy

The Tao says that money flows toward those who mentally attract it, and it flows away from inhospitable environments. It flows like water—hence the term *liquidity*—as it did when the Knights Templar created the modern-day banking system by opening branches through which their wealth flowed. The reason banks exist is because the Knights needed somewhere to store their silver and gold when they went into battle, and they wanted the pilgrims to be able to deposit gold in their home country and be able to withdraw gold at the Vatican to pay for their sins. Banking was created so that the cabal can get your money from you anytime, anywhere, or anyway they see fit. Money tucked away at home is of no good to those who rule over humanity.

Once you realize that money is fluid by nature, you can use it to your advantage. You can start to host it as a temporary custodian rather than as an "owner," which you never truly are. We don't really own money, despite what might be in our bank accounts. Those accounts simply house the money for you.

Money Flows to Those Who Know How to Use It

We need to learn to be able to treat money properly and host it well. You can start at zero and build a prudent reserve in a few months. People have amassed fortunes without ever planning or wanting to amass fortunes. Instead, they created some form of value that attracted money, which subsequently arrived. Money arrived as a *symptom* of doing something valuable.

For me, the more spiritual and grounded I tried to become, the better host I became for money—and being a host for money allows you to take pressure off. It gives you permission to find out who you might want to become or where you might want to focus your energy during your short existence. In the next chapter, we'll explore how you can be a better host for money.

Wealth Starts with You

Any problem that can be solved with money isn't a real problem.

We just need to learn to look at money in a different way, because the way most people see it is limited and often willfully ignorant. We put limits on our relationship with money and what it can do for us ... once we stop chasing it.

THE RIGHT MINDSET

In *The Big Leap* (2009), Gay Hendricks talks about what he calls the "upper limit problem." Everyone polishes up their résumés and then goes to apply for the job that's within the same bracket of income they just came from. We all have a set idea of what kind of income is right for us. It's the same with everything in life: from partners to cars, we have set expectations. Limits everywhere on everything.

We need to change that—and we can. As Wayne Dyer always said, "When you change the way you look at things, the things you look at change."

When I was eighteen, I was asked to apply for a very senior job I didn't think I'd get in a million years. I was underqualified and too young. I didn't even have the prerequisite certification, but I was also perfect for the job. So I got it, and I was made qualified after I was awarded it.

Just because you haven't done something yet doesn't mean you can't do it. Just because you haven't made $10,000 per day in the stock market doesn't mean you can't do it.

You have to remove the upper limit on your thinking. You need to figure out what will give you the best life without putting a band around it.

I used to believe that $100,000 a year was a big income. Then, when I made some money myself, I realized that a lot of people routinely make that as a monthly income but look and act just the same as you and me.

We can all do the same, but *only* if we give ourselves permission to imagine it. It has to start in the mind.

Thoughts → Feelings → Actions → Results

Give Yourself Permission

Our baseline sets our relationship with money. Change the way you look at things, and the things you look at change. You can think, "Shit, I'm broke," or you can think, "I'm not doing bad at all. I paid off all my debt this year, and that's a great place to be."

Immediately after I read *The Big Leap* a few years ago, I allowed myself to take Mondays off. Instead of thinking it was irresponsible or selfish, I changed how I looked at it. I thought, "Well, what if Monday became my mental health day or my exercise day?"

I gave myself permission, and it was a great decision.

We all tell ourselves stories over and over about what is possible. Those stories foster reality. We know that we manifest our own reality. When we think something, we put it out into the universe, and eventually we will physically pull it right into our reality. Thoughts are directly connected with the world. Your thoughts lead to feelings, your feelings lead to actions, and your actions lead to results.

If someone is having a really horrible experience right now, they shouldn't start with the results they want to achieve. They should start with their thoughts or feelings and see what actions they motivate. The results will come.

Create friction points, start small, and change the little things—and watch the big things start to take care of themselves.

Being healthy and happy is a function of your own doing; it is not something that modern medicine can help you with. As Aldous Huxley observed, "Medical science has made such tremendous progress that there is hardly a healthy human left."

Peaceful Capitalism

Zen Buddhism says people should learn to be fluid, like water. Water will instantly adapt to any shape perfectly without effort or exertion. It flows to the lowest points, so it has no hierarchy and is the ultimate in humility. It rules above all by being at the bottom. It is at peace and at ease. Water doesn't *do*; water simply *is*—it is at *ease*.

The opposite of *ease* is *dis-ease*. Disease is how we spell it now.

It relates to what I call peaceful capitalism. The common image of capitalism is all about taking, growing, being aggressive, being persistent. Buddhism is the opposite. It is about *being* and *allowing*.

The die-hard capitalist does nothing but endure. Even during the good days and months, he's thinking about the tax bill coming up. Most traders are quite neurotic, which seems to come with the territory. They live off caffeine and nicotine, they drink heavily, and they gamble—a lot, both at work and outside.

The peaceful capitalist realizes that life is meant to be *enjoyed, not endured*.

The more you are like water, the easier it will be to be at peace with any speculation or business decision. Water doesn't have to try to get a result. It just does the same thing every time, perfectly, effortlessly, silently.

I knew I had to bring the two worlds together—hard-charging capitalism and the fluidity of water—to create the harmony and balance to allow me to succeed.

In my youth, I had a front-row seat watching very compulsive, very negative, neurotic people who thought the worst thoughts, felt the worst feelings, did the worst things, and got the worst results. They didn't get the raise at work, then the guy who got the job buys a bigger house next door and rubs it in their face. They start to manifest all these different results because they never thought they were worthy of getting the job. They almost scripted mediocrity and suffering for themselves.

Control Your Thought Loops

A great subject for new traders and investors is neuro-linguistic programming: our thoughts create our feelings, which forge into action, which in turn gives us results.

Make sure you control that narrative in your mind. If you create a negative dialogue, you're going to get negative results.

The whole money mind starts with controlling your thoughts and feelings around money and your ability to earn it.

Like wealth to the positive thinker, poor decisions compound with the negative money mind. When some people find themselves in a deep depression and things aren't working, they think, "*Of course* I didn't get the job. *Of course* I didn't win the lottery. *Of course* I'm a victim."

Instead, they should stop and think, "I've been in a negative thought loop for weeks. It's no wonder the world around me appears to be not really working for me."

It's about expectations. If you fix your upper limit problem and expect something decent to happen to you, don't be surprised when it does. You *can* think good things into happening.

HOW YOU DO ANYTHING
IS HOW YOU DO EVERYTHING

Whenever I meet positive people, I ask them about their morning routine. The answer is always the same. They have a puppy-dog mentality in which they see each day as a blank page. Each morning, they ask themselves, "How do I want to write this page?"

They expect something good to happen. You can achieve the same positivity by pretending you have a documentary crew following you around, so you make your life fun and interesting. You can choose how little or how big your day will be.

Wake Up Whistling

It all starts with greeting the day instead of looking at the alarm and thinking, "Oh no." My grandfather got up whistling at 5:00 a.m. every morning. His attitude was that "every day is a good day to have a good day."

Positive people get up early and greet the day. My most successful periods came when I consistently got up early and got my arms around the day before it got around me. And the bad times came when I crawled out of bed late feeling anxious or stressed, and brushed my teeth quicker because I was already chasing the day. I'd try using substances to catch up, whether it was caffeine, nicotine, prescription pills, or narcotics, but those things shouldn't have a place in a professional trader's morning routine. They're self-perpetuating, and they make the whole situation a lot harder than it needs to be. If I drink too much at night, I sleep in and waste the day. I smoke pot to get my stomach better, and I end up going to bed late again due to bad food choices from the munchies.

For me to be productive, I can't get depressed, and to not be depressed I have to get up really early. By the time 10:00 p.m. rolls around, I'm tired enough to put my head down and pass right out. A proper sleep cycle is nature's antidepressant.

The obstacle is the way: if getting up early is not something that comes easy to you, perhaps that's exactly what you need to do to form a new habit loop. Let tons of other positive side effects of this new habit spill into your weeks and months.

Can you imagine if you had stock positions and you missed the opening of the markets and screwed up something really important, all because you were too lazy to crawl out of bed? That's a very sobering thought. It's something I have done an embarrassing amount of times while I was learning to trade.

Getting up early and owning the day is one of the greatest life hacks there is. You'll feel far less rushed and more in control. It only takes a few days to cement the habit.

The trick is to have something to look forward to in the morning, which could be a stock setup or could be some exercise that turns on all the systems in our body.

Aubrey Marcus wrote an entire book about how no one is in command of their life until they get up early, drink a gallon of water, do some stretches in the sun, and then say, "Okay, universe, now I am ready. Now I can be of service to others."

The 5AM Club by Robin Sharma (2018) helped me in that department. When I woke up before the markets opened, it had a profound effect on how I thought about my day. I'd take stuff for my body—water, magnesium, vitamin D, probiotics, and so on—and then I'd start to work on my portfolio, not the other way around.

Find when you function best and identify a stable routine. Calibrate your optimal time. It could be 5:00 a.m. or it could be 8:00 a.m. Do some testing to find it.

Before an independent investor takes their money into their own hands, they need to be healthy. In my early years on the markets, my life was in turmoil. I wondered why my account gyrated wildly from good to bad to sideways, but it was just a manifestation of my own life and habits.

You have to know what's right for you so you'll know if you're off track. Test your realities; diagnose yourself like you would a machine or tuning your guitar. It's about making small, consistent changes, like leaving your cell phone in another room overnight or placing the alarm on the other side of the bedroom so you have to walk to it in the morning.

Save yourself stress by knowing your limits and what you're trying to achieve. It's about finding your optimal place.

You're Starting a Relationship with an Addictive Substance

If you get into bed at a different time every day, and you check the same market at a different time every day, how are you ever going to sync into the market? If you trade commodities, you need to be at your screen at the same time every morning to see how things are trending hours before the open. If you're coming at it from all angles, it's all random. Nothing is going to be under control.

Figure out what affects your mood or behaviors, because it will affect your trading too. Trading is like entering into a relationship with a potentially destructive substance—money—and that's something you can't take lightly. If you don't really drink and you're going to start drinking tomorrow, you better have some firm rules in place so that alcohol won't get the best of you. It's the same with gambling or with shopping. If you're going to get in the money game, you're starting a relationship with an addictive substance. I've learned, for example, that I trade far better when I've not been smoking weed. Weed makes me incredibly passive with stocks and light-footed with money. In the markets, you need to be assertive, so I have to push my date with Mary Jane to after the bell if I want to be most effective at my job.

Same goes for caffeine: I like it thirty minutes before the opening bell to give myself the most focus and energy I can for the first hour. I then taper off mentally and try to trade less after about 7:30–8:00 a.m. (PST). By 9:00 a.m. on the West Coast, more than half of all market participants are already at lunch on the East Coast, so be advised of these types of traffic patterns and know where you fit in best.

Strangely enough, it was psilocybin mushrooms, aka "magic mushrooms," that ultimately unlocked my freedom by way of self-love. I wouldn't recommend them for everyone, but they gave me the insight that my desire to please others and not rock the boat was causing chaos in my life. I decided *I* was worthwhile too. To stop lighting myself on fire to keep others warm—to be my own man.

Anyone who wants to make that step needs to have enough self-love and self-respect to remove the chaos around them. They need to treat their business like a job, because as an independent, you're on your own. There's no one else to tell you when you're doing a good or bad job, no one to smack you over the head. Stop trying to please others, and start pleasing yourself by muting out the unnecessary or unhelpful noise.

If you do the right thing, the right outcome will happen. As they say in *Fight Club*, "It's only after you've lost everything that you're free to do anything." In other words, you have to experience the bottom to know what the top feels like.

Try to detach from outcomes. Your wife might leave you tomorrow, but you can love her today. Your job might suck, but it's already lunchtime . . . and tonight will be great. You're in a trade that's not working, but you can go for a walk in the sunshine.

Don't let the anticipated outcome cloud your judgment. Detaching from outcomes is freedom.

You're looking at your trade, and today it might be up or it might be down. What about over the whole month? What about the quarter? What about the year? Sometimes you need to sit back and zoom out a little. Get away from the screen and see the broader picture.

If you're not in the right mindset, that's a good decision. In the right mindset, you can use a hammer to build a beautiful house. In the wrong mindset, you can use it to destroy. So if you're feeling destructive, back away and go get your head right.

Focus on the 5 Percent You Can Control

We're deceiving ourselves if we think we're in full control of our lives. Take driving as an example. You get in your car and turn the ignition. You don't control if it will start or not. You put it into gear, and you don't control if the transmission will work. You don't control if you'll get a flat tire or not. You don't control the traffic, nor the lights or patterns, nor the weather, nor the closures, nor the animals on the road. All you can control are the direction and the throttle, which is less than 5 percent of the driving equation.

Most things we face are uncontrollable, yet people seem to put most of their effort and mental energy into uncontrollables like the weather, rather than their speed or direction.

That attitude helps me to be accepting of things. It means I keep my focus, my attention, and my energy on the tiny percent I can control.

Keep your bandwidth for things you have an influence over.

Keep the Same Demeanor

Hang out with people you admire who are living the lives you want, not those whose lifestyle you are trying to escape. When you do, don't just take from the ambience; try and add to it. Strive to be the dumbest person in the room so that you can learn from everyone else. If you want to be interesting to people who are wealthier than you, be a beacon of light. Smile, because people want to know why you're smiling. It makes them interested in you.

The old business adage says, "In the room, in the deal." In other words, if people start talking about a new deal, and you're at the table, you might even get asked to join in. Because you're there, even if you're the lowest person on the totem pole. Put yourself out there with people who are just a few years ahead of you. They'll often appreciate the acknowledgment and are usually surprisingly helpful if you ask.

Have the comfort to put yourself out there and ask. You can go to Starbucks and strike up a conversation with somebody that has a Swiss watch on. It's cheesy and painful, but it can be as simple as, "I love your watch."

"Oh, thanks for noticing that." Next thing you know, they give you a business card and say, "I'm looking for help on something."

If you want to be better, seek out betterment. Don't be so caught up in yourself that you assume that other people don't want anything to do with you.

Know What Is Important and What Is Irrelevant

Acceptance is the answer to all of life's problems. Get a grip. Be aware of what is important to you versus what is irrelevant. Choose your battles.

A bad gambler hoots and hollers when he wins, and moans and grumbles when he loses. You're a lot more dangerous out there when you're always smiling. Keep people guessing. Have grace. Be a decent person.

Think of James Bond in the casino. He puts down his chips and loses, but he just grins and nods and walks away. He doesn't bang on the table or protest to the croupier. You have to have that same sort of energy when you're trading, because you can't always bet red and win. Sometimes black comes up, and you have to be able to face it and stay suave.

In the investment world, grace is one of the most underappreciated commodities.

LEARN FROM OTHERS

Always stay honest and speak your truth. This is where the rubber meets the road. Anyone who is a bullshitter or afraid to speak up makes a situation worse. Your life will ultimately be easier if you remain authentic and communicate your true feelings. When I was young, I was always too afraid of the outcome to speak my truth. I paid a steep price for that.

People Don't Care What You Know until They Know Why You Care

All it takes is clear and honest communication. If you go to an accountant and say, "I've always wondered this," or you ask a lawyer, "I always wondered that," people are remarkably willing to help. If they understand why you're asking what you're asking, they're often willing to stop, put the pen down, and actually help you. Because your request came from a sincere place, most people won't just ignore it, and no one will think you're stupid.

It's the same when you reach out to people on Twitter or YouTube.

The web is full of information. If you were to Google any component of the investing or trading world, you'll find a hundred videos about any one small part of the process. So there's never an excuse to say, "I don't know how all that works." There's many hundreds of thousands of hours of free stock market education online.

And for the most part, it's reliable. Most of the early information I needed in my journey I learned from short articles on Investopedia. What is a proxy battle? What does it mean when an activist investor takes a stake in a company, shows up at the annual general meeting, and tries to throw the board? Ask yourself the question, and an hour later, you'll know the answer. They don't teach you that in school, but the professionals and the MBAs learn it, so do-it-yourselfers need to teach themselves. Now when I see a press release of a dissident investor, I know exactly what's going on behind the scenes. And it was just one little article that got me up to speed on what became a fascination with corporate raiders like Carl Icahn, the so-called activist investors.

Google is your friend. Whenever people ask me, "What the heck does that mean, anyway?" I send them a link to a site called LMGTFY (Let Me Google That for You) just to remind them that everything is on there.

Keep the Faith

Make others feel good about you and themselves. If you're confident, others will be confident in you. We're all joined together as part of the hive mind. We see ourselves as unique snowflakes, but we're all just bundles of seven trillion cells moving in step like schools of fish or flocks of birds. It's a *Homo sapien* phenomenon to dye our hair blue and pierce our noses to make ourselves "unique," but we're all part of the hive. By making others feel good, you make yourself feel good. We are quite literally the same organism on the surface of this blue rock hurtling through space and time. Strange surface creatures living at the bottom of an ocean of air.

We're all sending and receiving energy, and if you want good energy coming in, you need to send out authenticity and love. You need to live and let live, love and be loved. Effective communication is the key to making it all work. When you communicate poorly, things are going to spiral. One wrong yes can lead to so many problems. If you say, "Okay, I'll do that" when you know you shouldn't, you're not respecting yourself. You're being inauthentic, dishonest, and not loving. Doing things out of fear is the opposite of love.

You have to believe in yourself and what you're capable of, but you also have to know what you're doing. If someone comes to me and says, "I'm going to be rich," I don't laugh because I know anyone *can* become rich. So I say to them, "Okay. Walk me through it." Most people can't.

Strong belief will get you through fear, which comes as standard for a trader in the markets. Reassure yourself with the old proverb:

"Fear knocked on the door. Faith answered. There was no one there." If you have faith in the process and faith in your own intuition, the fear will disappear. The anticipation is the worst part. As Mark Twain said, "I've been through some terrible things, some of which actually happened."

Live Well and Roll with the Punches

Your definition of a good life will depend on your circumstances, but holding yourself accountable for certain standards, taking care of yourself and others, and having stable reference points all contribute to living well. It's a package deal. There are lots of miserable rich people, but the ones who are happy tend to have pretty rigid rules but seemingly remain very flexible. Even the most flamboyant ones—like Richard Branson—get up at the same time each day, have the same breakfast, and follow the same exact schedule: they have to. But they also know when they need to be flexible, like a palm tree that can bend all the way to the ground in a hurricane. Its flexibility is also its strength. Its flexibility keeps it alive.

Your plan needs to be flexible enough to survive a hurricane.

Be able to roll with the punches. Stay fluid, like water (you are 60 percent water), so you can go with the flow. Don't try to make too much happen. Don't paddle too far upstream. Drowning victims actually drown because of exhaustion from unnecessary flailing. They exhaust themselves at a time when all they need to do is completely surrender. Instead, lie on your back, stay calm, and you will effortlessly float.

It's the struggle that kills us.

You need to have confidence in the markets before you start, because it's all about real-time self-control. It's about not panicking when shit goes sideways and not getting too greedy if it all looks a bit too easy. It's about getting up every day, sticking to your routine with a sort of religious discipline.

All of my best trading months were the ones that I met the opening bell ready and prepared for that day. I was *immutable*, so money freely flowed into my ecosystem of doing the same thing each day.

Say your neighbors come over for a beer, and next thing you know it's 1:30 a.m., and you're doing shots, and you miss work the next day. You knew you shouldn't have, but you were easily swayed. If you go into the market and are easily convinced, you're going to be like a ship in the ocean getting banged around wave after wave. Rudderless and directionless.

You're going to sink.

Be Ready to Make Consistent Sound Decisions

There's no room for self-loathing if you want to take control of your money. You need full confidence and self-control. There are serious decisions to make every day, and if you're not ready for them, you will do more harm than good. Even if you have a good month, you'll have one bad day, and you'll blow it all up. You're either advancing or you're coasting, and you can only coast downhill.

It's a balance between self-respect and being flexible enough to be humble and accepting every time you're wrong. Which you will be at times, by the way. It's all in how you handle it. It's "going the course" and not changing the plan just because of an unexpected loss or change.

The best advice I can give new traders is to start paper trading. Track your proposed investments with a pen and a pad for a few weeks at a minimum until you start to see patterns, until you turn naivete and inexperience into confidence. There are online accounts now where you can do paper trading in a simulated account so you don't even have to write anything down. You can start to see how you would do if you had $100,000 of real capital working for you in the markets. What would it look like in thirty days?

Sooner or later, you'll switch from thinking, "Wow, I'm glad I only did that on paper," to "Wow, I'm actually making good decisions here. Maybe it's time to trade for real."

We've spent some time exploring your relationship with money. Now it's time to trade. Let's look more closely at the stock market and how it works.

PART 2

YOUR MONEY

Plan Your Trade and Trade Your Plan

Bad trades happen all the time, whether it's a $10,000 bet on Bitcoin, an overnight stock flip for $30,000, or $15 million to purchase a franchise. Not everything works out. You can't avoid it completely, but you can minimize it by knowing what you're getting into and knowing *exactly* when you plan to get out.

It's been true as long as traders have been trading. That's why we still use the ancient Roman phrase *Caveat emptor*: "Buyer beware." It's *your* duty to know what *you're* doing. If you don't take responsibility for what you're getting into, no one else will. If you're about to make a trade or cut a check, and you're not sure why you're doing it or what you're buying, or you feel a twinge in your gut, hold back.

The first rule of trading is plan your trade and trade your plan. It means simply this: make sure you have a damn good, explainable and understandable reason to enter the trade or investment (a *great* reason is even better). Have a strategy. And set an entry price and a target exit price—for above and below your entry—before you buy anything. Map it out *before* you set sail.

It's a simple rule to explain, but it's not so easy to follow because we're human beings, and we have emotions. By the time I was crawling back to the weed business in Vegas every week, whatever had attracted me to the investment in the first place had long gone, and I didn't want anything to do with it. Every fiber in my being told me not to do this, but emotion, fear, and FOMO kept pulling me back, first in the shape of someone I looked up to who persuaded me to throw out my plan and also thanks to my own natural instinct to try to please people.

That's something that's blown me off course time after time. In this case, it was a three-year detour for breaking my first rule of having a clearly defined entry and exit plan before you take action.

KNOW WHAT YOU *WANT* FROM A TRADE

Your strategy depends on making sure you know what you want from the trade. Say you intend to double your money. If you buy a stock at $10 with a target price of $20, then when it hits $20, you sell. No ifs, ands, or buts. You don't sit and wonder if it might go up to $25. It's done its job, as have you, so you're out. If you're tempted to stay in, sure, it might go to $25, but the next day, you could easily be down to $15, having given up half of what you'd have gotten had you stuck to the plan.

If this keeps happening to you, you're going to hate your life and wonder why you're failing. You're playing the game completely wrong.

It's not enough just *having* a plan. You have to trade it exactly as prescribed. Don't throw your roadmap out the window once greed or fear get the better of you: emotion and moving prices don't mix. It's not always easy. If you buy a thousand shares, and the share price goes up a dollar, it sometimes takes a lot of willpower to get back out again—or sit tight—depending on what the plan is. You're up over $1,000 on the day; the dollar signs are flashing in your eyes. Maybe you can do it again tomorrow? Maybe, but the statistical likelihood is that you won't. The numbers are greatly stacked against it happening. The next day, you'll be wondering why it's back below your price and hating your life decisions again. It might be a month before it turns green again. Maybe longer.

Take your profit and get out. You've reached your goal. If the price triples afterward, it doesn't matter! You can't always have your fishing line in every little pool of water. I often hear people complain that they *left a lot on the table*, but it's utter nonsense. Once you're no longer a player, it doesn't matter what's left on the table! It's not worth a damn worrying about tables you're *not on*, because you can't be on them all.

Losing Hurts Way More Than Winning Feels Good

It's all a question of mindset. Old-time gamblers avoid losing, even if it means getting out before the top of the market. Setting realistic targets and being content to reach them is the heart of planning your trade.

The professional gambler takes his $100,000 and aims to make $10,000, a modest 10 percent return. The amateur walks into the picture with $10,000 and shoots to make $100,000, which is a 1,000 percent gain. That's a moon shot, and it's highly unlikely. Who do you think will achieve their goal?

Try to get away from this amateur mindset of going in small and hoping to make it out huge. When you flip it around the right way, you can start to see how repeated base hits can create fortunes. Very few people can knock it out of the park, and almost no one does it over a long period of time.

Planning your trade helps avoid one of the worst feelings you can have in the markets: becoming an accidental investor on a short-term trade. You buy a stock on a tip from your long-lost second cousin-in-law, and it goes against you, but you're too afraid to accept defeat and take the loss, so now you're just hanging out, potentially forever against your own will. If someone asks why you own the stock, you tell them you "didn't mean to." It was inadvertent. You took a swing for the fences, the fences weren't there, and now you're an *involuntary investor*. Being able to recognize this is powerful, and it will save you years of torture.

If a trade goes against you and you failed to create a solid plan around a stop loss, it will turn you into an "involuntary investor," a term first used by Jesse Livermore, the American stock trader and main character of the classic book I've already mentioned, *Reminiscences of a Stock Operator*. You'll watch that position fall day after day, and it's going to fuck up your mindset when it comes to future trades. It's a millennium-old common rookie mistake. Throw a few thousand bucks at an opportunity that doesn't go well, then stick with it. If you've only got $10,000 and each swing costs $1,000, you've got ten goes. The math says you'll need far more chances than that. It's the easiest and most common way to blow up an amateur trading account.

INVESTMENT AND SPECULATION

Buying shares on the market comes in two forms: investing, usually with a long-term outlook, and speculating, usually for a short-term win. They are not the same thing. When someone "invests" in a company's common stock, their outlook should be upward of five or more years. If you're a speculator chasing momentum or seasonal trends, your trading outlook can be as short as five minutes. That kind of position is called a "trade." It's not something you're married to. An investment, on the other hand, is something that people really want to have in their portfolios, to the extent that if it goes up enough for them to sell it, they'll likely buy it again at some point in the future.

The key difference is time. When someone is investing, they shouldn't care what the price does in the short term. It's a very freeing position. If I'm buying Energy Co at $30 and I plan to give the shares to my children, I could care less if it goes to $28 the next day. But if I'm a speculator, I'm underwater and potentially in trouble.

Investing is freeing because the real value of your holding is detached from the current cost. You can be completely detached from the outcome, at least for a year or more, while it does its thing. Once you own it, you own it. You don't really care about your monthly statements; you care about owning the asset over time. If you're speculating, you care about the price every single day. You have to.

Which Hat Are You Comfortable Wearing?

Investing and speculating are two different vocations. You need to figure out which one you're more comfortable doing. For some people, the daily gyrations of the market make them feel a bit sick. Most stocks can experience huge pricing fluctuations and volatility, whipping people in and out at the wrong time. When the price goes down, speculators despair and get out, but the investors who bought the good names use the low price to buy more shares "on sale."

A speculator rents shares (or sells them short) for profit, while an investor owns a small piece of the underlying company. The speculator doesn't concern himself with the operations and nuances of the underlying company. The investor cares deeply and should spend an hour or more a week keeping themselves informed of the company they own.

Speculation in the hope of price appreciation requires timing and the faith that you can find a greater fool. Investment is more systematic. Say you own 0.001 percent of Lululemon and you want to increase your shareholdings until you own .01 percent of the company. You buy some of it in the $30s, some in the $50s, even some in the $100s. It doesn't really matter, because you're accumulating for the long term. If you invest in a stock at $10 per share, and the very next month, it falls to $5, you should be pleased. Now you can buy more of the company at a 50 percent discount from last month.

As the stock market saying goes, BTFD: buy the fucking dip.

Alternatively, if you're looking to flip for income, then buying at $10 and falling to $5 means you've lost half of your position. You could have implemented a loss stop at 10 percent, or $9, but instead you gave up 50 percent of your whole position because you didn't pay attention to your exposure.

You may never get back to $10, no matter how long you wait. Once you're at $5, you need to make 100 percent just to break even, which is statistically almost impossible near term.

It sounds obvious, but if it was, then traders would never let their stock holdings fall by 50 percent. Investors, meanwhile, don't mind as long as the value thesis is still intact. It's freeing, but it needs conviction and a long-term outlook.

But it avoids being left holding a hot potato.

WHAT AM I DOING HERE?

Every independent trader needs a trading journal.

There are many books one can read about the market, but none are as important as the one you write yourself. A trading journal is a critical tool. I've been using one for over fifteen years and would be lost without it. It's where you plan your trade. It's your map, your ledger, your everything. It keeps emotion out of your trading and lets you see your thoughts.

I started mine because I got sick of getting whipsawed back and forth in the markets. I decided that I wouldn't keep flirting with trading. I sat down for about six months and did nothing but read all of the good trading books I could get my hands on. Then I digested what I'd learned into a page of ten commandments. I've followed them ever since. They're imprinted on the back of my retinas, and they've provided for my loved ones and me.

I have an ongoing digital journal that I add a sentence or two to every single day. It tracks the bigger things, high and low points. Anything notable. Then I have my physical journal, which is for the bigger picture. I open it about once a month and write half a page about where I am in the universe: how many shares I hold of this or what I want to start to accumulate more of. I have both a micro and a macro journal at all times.

Each Friday I look back and think, "Here's where I made money this week; here's where I lost money." If I don't stop for five minutes to write it down, I won't carry that knowledge into the next week. I regularly review how I've done week by week and month by month.

Keeping a journal helps you identify patterns. You go back and think, I did this before, how did I do it a second time? I'm not going to do it a third time. The journal insulates me from making the same mistake two or three times.

One of the major functions of the journal is gratitude. It's almost like saying, "Today was a good day, *thank you*. I made $6,000 on a $50,000 trade I started last week. I knew it was right from the outset, and it was perfectly executed."

That makes me smile inside. It helps me to take time to be grateful for the wins and to reinforce that I do know what I'm doing. It's better than flying by the seat of your pants. When you sit down with your accountant at the end of the year, it's good to have some sense of where you gained and where you lost and why. Anything else is not investing, it's blind gambling.

I still make stock mistakes from time to time. Fewer than I used to, but I still make them. And I flip through my notes and see that it's part of a pattern. The journal makes all mistakes valuable, because it turns them into teaching experiences. As soon as you realize that you buy the volatility index (VIX) every summer because you're sure the market's going to crash, and then it doesn't, maybe it's time to reassess that particular plan.

My paper journal enables me to identify my trends in critical areas. I saw that I chopped gainers the same day that I would add to, and hold, my losers. I'd give up $30,000 positions that hit $31,000 to buy more of the $30,000 positions that were currently worth $25,000. I repeated it for years until I unlocked the issue in my journal. I was buying then selling the same day, only to buy back in again the next day with mood changes. I was creating more motion in the ocean than necessary. I was my portfolio's own worst enemy.

The reason I still keep a physical journal—which seems pretty quaint in today's electronic world—is that at 8:00 p.m. on a Monday night or Tuesday night, I can just open it up, look at tomorrow's date, and then create three bullet items and empty check boxes. And when I go in at 6:30 a.m., and I can't even think what day it is, let alone remember everything from the night before, I have three little to-dos right there looking at me before I do anything else. I never leave myself thinking, "What did I forget to do?"

The journal gives you data hindsight, pattern recognition, and justification of movement, which is growth. The act of writing it down helps you to codify your memory. I close out my brokerage account on screen, I write a couple of sentences in my journal, and then I put a period on the day.

Parallel but Opposite Rules

Investing is a vacation. It's totally feet up and laid back. You can do it at work or in your spare time. It doesn't require any effort other than the research on what you want to own. Once you own the investment, you can be hands-off.

If you are looking for income by way of speculation, the commitment is much greater, it's a lot of work. They're light years apart, so approach them differently.

To take myself as an example, I don't particularly like to *invest* in stocks; I prefer to invest in my mind, my kids, our health, real estate, businesses. I don't invest in things that carry the risk of potentially devastating near-term losses, flash crashes, bank failures, debt bubbles, inept policy makers, or anything else.

I use the stock market like a gambler uses the casino or a handicapper treats the pony track.

The rules are parallel but opposite. If you're an investor and the stock falls, you buy more. If you're a trader and the stock falls, you sell before it destroys too much capital.

Even on a good trade, a trader will often be tempted to close the position early because greed or fear kicks in, and he wants to sell to realize or "lock in" the gain. Everyone has done it. It can be a lot harder to sit on your hands when you can see that your trade has already gone up handsomely. That's what disciplined traders do. They chop their losses quickly and let their winners run according to the plan.

Whenever you look at your market position and ask yourself, "What am I doing here?" go back to your journal and find the day you made the trade. If you wrote that Costco is the best retailer in the world, period, and you want to own some of it forever, then if the market crashes, you can refer back to your journal and think, "Okay. I told myself I'm going to want it forever. I'll get through this." You can accept the consequences of your decision. You can see what has gone well and decide what you might have to reassess.

Trade, Investment, Trade

In January 2020, I started buying a small unknown cannabis company called Experion Holdings at an $8 million valuation, I bought it every week for twelve months. In January of 2021, a full year later, it started to pop. It doubled and then doubled again. A quadruple inside thirteen months. By now, my goal was to own 5 percent of this tiny undiscovered business that I really liked and that I knew inside and out. But when it doubled too quickly, it passed the point of value for me.

The stock became too expensive too fast, so I had to be flexible. In this case, my plans had to change on the fly. When it became overvalued, I got out and never looked back at the now overpriced asset.

Experion changed its name to Citizen Stash once it got some popularity, and then Valens, a much larger company, offered to buy Citizen Stash in August of 2021 for $54 million. In typical stock market fashion, buyers who didn't want to own it at an $8 million valuation a year earlier with the same amount of sales and assets lined up to buy it at the new $54 million price tag. The completion of the acquisition was finalized on November 8, 2021.

Not only was the company way overvalued; it was losing $1 million a quarter and had to take on a private mortgage to keep the lights on and try to promote the stock.

It's the definition of a hot potato. No wonder the board took the very first buy-out offer.

For me, Experion began as a swing trade, then became more of an investment as my position grew, and ultimately became a trade again as performance outpaced my expectations.

In a case like that, I keep going back to my journal and checking my plan, then run the numbers and decide if the deal still has something to offer me. When Experion was eight cents, it was only an $8 million market cap company (market capitalization: its value based on the share price multiplied by the amount of shares outstanding), which was cheap enough for me to see a no-brainer opportunity for a double. It was undervalued by half, based on my months of due diligence and multiple visits to the site and conversations with its CEO and chairman of the board. When it went to a $30 million market cap, it was overvalued by at least double in my eyes, with roughly $16 million in total assets at that time.

The prospect went from buying the company at *50 cents on the dollar* to owning shares that were priced at *over 200 percent* of the company's net asset value. Plus, it now had debt on its building and land. Therefore, I no longer saw it as something that I *needed* to own. It doubled in value, and my approach of "buying value" was no longer applicable. I had bought it every single week for over a year. If it was still that low, I'd still be buying it today, because I actually wanted to own the company long term for several reasons. But as soon as all the parameters changed and it got too expensive, I didn't want it anymore—I could not justify holding it. The reasons no longer mattered because the valuation was now wrong. When you go from $8 million to $54 million in one year, the greater fool theory compresses even further. In other words, if you get too greedy and don't take your gains and move on, in a case like this, you might just be the one left holding the bag if and when the music stops.

Averaging Down Is Excellent—
Until It's the Kiss of Death

Failure to plan is certain death. That's one of the few certainties in stock trading. Take averaging down, which is one of the most controversial subjects in the investing world. Averaging down is buying more stock you already own when its current price drops below your cost or initial buy level. That way, you reduce the average price you've paid per share. There are times when it makes sense, but it's also often the kiss of death because you might be throwing good money after bad.

Say you trade Tesla by buying shares long at $700. It goes to $600, and you buy more, then $500, and you buy even more. Then an accounting scandal comes out, and the price tanks to under $300—but you're still buying it. Why are you still averaging down when the stock is getting wiped out? You'll be left with a position worth nothing. You are trying to catch a falling dagger, so you better be practicing sound asset allocation in terms of how many chips you are willing to keep putting on the table with the hand you are holding.

The proper term for averaging down the right way is known as dollar-cost averaging, which is stretching out your purchase of an asset over time in small, regular buys, whether the asset is going up or down, which is a potent tool for investors. If you're investing long term in an exchange-traded fund (ETF) with a basket of various stocks, and you're bullish on natural gas and oil, then every month, you put $500 into an energy ETF. That kind of dollar-cost averaging allows you to take advantage of any dips in the price while also protecting you against buying too much at once if the price is currently too high.

Averaging down on the fly while your trade is going against you is completely different. A lot of trading books discuss it, but it's the quickest and easiest way to reduce the value of your portfolio. You're not going to last long if you are a reckless catcher of falling daggers. Take a trader who speculates on gold using long-term call options. If the position goes south when he's trying to play to the upside, and he keeps buying at a lower price to average down, he's throwing good money after bad. He's doubling down when he should be getting out.

Don't Sell Your Winners to Buy Your Losers

It's the easiest way to reduce the value of your portfolio. It's a common mistake I see with rookie and seasoned traders alike.

Everyone sooner or later sells their winners to buy their losers. They sell stocks that are green to finance the purchase of the stocks that have gone red on them. It's human nature, but it means they've forgotten their plan. They've confused a trade with an investment. Or worse, they don't know what they want. They're flailing instead of surrendering, just like a drowning victim.

Averaging down or dollar-cost-averaging an investment you aim to keep in the long run is a sound practice; adding more to a position that has gone against you to try to lower your cost or get back to even is an amateur mistake.

It's very difficult not to buy something you just bought if you can get it cheaper. But then it goes down again, and now you're in the trap. It's happened to me countless times.

To Avoid the Trap, Paper-Trade First

The best traders out there paper-trade as a back test to see how they would have done in a simulated environment before they put capital to work. Say I want to buy gold. I can go back twenty years and check the price action in the first six months of the year versus the last six months of the year. Then I can get a snapshot of whether to buy gold in May or wait until September. It's based on twenty years of data—that's why the charts exist. They can't tell you the future, but they can tell you the history so you can make an informed decision. People want to try and predict the right side of the chart, which is the unknown future. And they forget to study the left side of the chart, which never lies.

Understand the Game

For most traders who want to step in and out smoothly with minimal liquidity risk, it's better to stick to the big exchanges, like the S&P 500. Once you're in the junior markets, you're often playing in illiquid pools, which means you can get trapped when you can't find a greater fool to take your hot potato from you. On the big exchanges, the likelihood of you getting stuck due to a lack of liquidity is virtually nonexistent.

Pick a company from the S&P 500 and get to know it. Paper-trade it. Choose something you understand so that when you read their news releases or look at their website, you know what they mean. It could be agriculture, personal healthcare, tech, or automotive. Having a basic understanding is part of getting an edge.

That's the reason I don't bet on sports. For one thing, I have no way to try to handicap, say, LeBron James versus Steph Curry. Also, I don't care, which is critically important. So to bet on it would be stupid; I don't have an edge, and I don't even want to learn the edge. Stick to what you care about. If you despise the US military indus-trial complex don't trade Boeing, Lockheed Martin, and Raytheon. But if you go to McDonald's for your Big Mac every day, that could be a wonderful stock for you since you're fully bought into the product they hawk. If you love McDonald's, you can start trading a company that you already know. Same goes for Apple or Google.

That's how I started out. I was eighteen and working in IT for the oil giant Suncor, and I thought, "I'm going to get to know this com-pany, because I buy gasoline every single week. I'm stuck spending a hundred bucks on nat gas and other fossil fuel products monthly, so I might as well buy the backend of it and profit there, while spending on the front end. And when it goes up in price, I'll be happy, not disappointed, because I bet against an outcome I don't want, in this case, higher oil prices."

I created an *emotional hedge* and educated myself about arbitrage in the energy markets.

Don't jump in too soon. You need significant practice and rep-etition behind the scenes before you're ready to show up to the big game, at which point you'll be taking on the professionals from the very first moment.

HOW DID I GET INTO THIS?

My dad never wanted to be a father, and then he became a dad of three. He fell into it inadvertently, it tore him up, and chaos ensued. He could have been at home relaxing with years of income saved and invested. Instead he started a family when his wife wanted to, not when he wanted to. *He set himself on fire to keep others warm.* He was not cut out for the role or its responsibilities. Every fiber in his body told him not to do it, and yet he went along with it like a leaf in the wind.

It was the same for me in Vegas. I planned to get out of the trade, but I broke the plan for some prominent, older male figures who were all invested and desperate to find a qualified CEO. I set myself on fire to please others because they were figures I looked up to, which made me even more eager to please them. A part of me was hopeful that I could fix their problem and get a pat on the back.

I was breaking one of the first rules of business: say *no*, and say it often.

It's the same thing on a trade. If you buy and it goes lower, you try to be a hero and keep it going by putting bids in and buying more as it falls lower. It doesn't help anybody. All it does is show a lack of self-love and discipline. It outs you as someone trying to be the hero.

Save yourself; don't do it. Wait for the good opportunities.

SOLAR ENERGY

In early 2010, I read a convincing article about the growing need for solar-energy solutions, which supported something I had been saying for years. I did some research to find a stock I could speculate on in the near term to take advantage of the growing demand for solar and what I thought was a near-term spike in interest in solar stocks (the greater fool theory). The most attractive was the cheapest, and that should have set the alarm bells ringing right off the bat. Oftentimes, the cheapest option looks more attractive because you can buy more shares; however, statistically you are far better off simply finding the biggest or second-biggest option in the general field, which has more probability of performing well on the upside and gives you more protection to the downside.

The shares were about $0.80, so I bought my first 250,000, planning that if they ticked up to around a dollar within two months, I could make an effortless 20 percent gain. However, as soon as I bulldozed into the market, early investors came out of the woodwork to take their chance to cash in as my buying suddenly became their unexpected liquidity event. The sudden small surge in this otherwise dormant stock saw it drop about 10 cents, so I bought another 100,000 shares at $0.69.

I now owned 350,000 shares in this "promising" solar venture because I had allowed greed to get the better of me. Everything I read and heard validated my hunch that solar was on the way up, so I just assumed I would come out of it all right. I was a greedy pig wanting something the easy way. I was seeking confirmation bias everywhere.

When the price hit $0.45 a month later, I bought more shares to "average down" my overall price. I now owned a half million shares, so I reached out to the CEO to get some reassurance that I had made a wise decision. When we spoke, he told me, "We'll be golden! Just keep buying. We'll be *very* good. Private jets to the AGM next year."

No joke, the CEO boasted to me on our very first call that we will make so much on this company that we'll be flying private to next year's annual meeting. This is classic penny stock bullshit.

Everything he said validated my ideas. Everything he said triggered my greed to buy yet more shares. Now my ego had taken over. I wanted to feel a part of something special. I wanted to be able to say, "I own a million shares of something."

I was no longer a trader of this ticker. I was now an involuntary investor in a fledgling startup company. I had drunk the Kool-Aid, a surefire way to die.

I'd shelved the plan thanks to a combination of greed and FOMO. Those emotions prevented me from looking at my position versus my plan. I had tied up most of my liquid capital in a million shares with a cost basis of around $0.75, allowing for a little averaging down. But the shares were trading at $0.40, which was a significant loss on paper—and the loss only got worse when the company ran out of money, as typically happens with penny stocks.

To raise money, they issued new shares in what is called a "private placement" at $0.45. Increasing the overall number of shares available in the company diluted the value of my holdings even more. I'd gone from owning 1 million shares out of 25 million to owning 1 million shares out of 40 million. I had significantly less of the overall pie, and I was losing money each week, and yet I stayed thanks to fear and greed.

The market capitalization was now $16 million, and it had been $10 million when I started.

It was getting overvalued.

Due Diligence Means What It Says

The disadvantage of the generally loose exchange regulations on penny stocks allow management to pull all kinds of money-raising stunts to keep the party going. Most at-home investors using online brokerage accounts might not even realize that the share count is increasing as often as every month. For every share creation the company does, the percentage of your holding is reduced, and the company becomes more expensive despite the share price remaining static.

There are only two answers to the problem beyond regulation about specific disclosure on dilution between reporting periods. Better governance by good independent directors who are legally tasked with preventing bad or inexperienced management decisions. And better due diligence by retail investors.

And when I say better due diligence, I don't mean checking Reddit or StockTwits.

If you see a share price deteriorate over time and assume the business is getting cheaper, there is always a chance that the market cap is staying the same or even increasing because the company is constantly issuing more shares in order to pay bloated management salaries.

Less than five months after my first investment in the solar business, when the private placement sellers were allowed to offer their shares, the price fell to $0.25, but the market cap was still near where it had been many months before at a much higher price per share. I had blown myself up with my own naivete and greed. I'd tried to people-please the unrealistically optimistic and cunning CEO. And I'd loved the ego trip of telling other people about my "big position" in a sexy new green technology.

That big position was now worth half what I had paid for it. I'd had a plan, but I hadn't stuck to it.

Optics Disguise All Sorts of Problems with New Businesses

That wasn't where the lesson ended. As bad as it was that I bought a company near a dollar and didn't sell when it went below a quarter, I hung on through a rollback of the shares. Simply put, a rollback is when a company that's in trouble reverse-splits its shares. If a company has 100 million shares and its price falls to $0.05 a share, it might reduce those shares, say 10 to 1, so it now has 10 million shares trading at $0.50.

A forward split works the same way but produces more shares, which are therefore cheaper, although the market cap remains the same. Tesla did it when their shares got up over $1,000 dollars, which started to make it look far too expensive—which it was. They split the shares so the price appeared to fall to the uneducated, and many noobs were deceived into thinking that the new price was far more attractive than it had previously been. In fact, it's already climbed back over that $1,000 mark per share again and more than tripled in value since the split. In other words, the deceitful practice worked.

Nothing has changed except the amount of shares. It's like slicing a pizza. You can cut it into quarters and you each get one piece, or you cut it into eight pieces and you each get two. It's still the same amount and weight of pizza split up in a different ratio.

Rollbacks happen in the junior markets all the time, and naive investors might not even notice anything beyond the steep selling that often follows. It's optics. It's a form of deception. A dirty little tool of the trade.

If a CEO is going around town trying to sell a private placement in his company at $0.50 per share with 10 million shares outstanding, the optics are more attractive than offering $0.05 a share with 100 million shares outstanding. In both cases, he's selling the shares with the exact same $5 million market cap. One looks polished and one looks loose, but they are identical.

Cap table restructuring to make an idea more financeable is a deceptive trick that you often see in the penny stock world.

It's completely legal if the directors vote on it on the grounds that it makes the most sense for the health and well-being of the business to roll back its shares. It's all for perception or attractability. Lipstick on a pig. They don't want the share price to look too low. The opposite is true on Wall Street. When a big company's shares get too expensive, a forward split creates more shares and lowers the stock price, which looks cheaper at a glance, and lures in more unsophisticated fish.

Optics matter. It's just like the $0.99 price point: two digits rather than three, but ultimately still $1.00.

The Market Really Is 90 Percent Smoke and Mirrors

The market is all about perceived value, with companies working hard to create and sustain a public image. If you can get behind the scenes, maybe at the AGM or at a board meeting, you often get a better view. Perhaps you learn that none of the directors are very educated on the business, maybe none of them like each other—in many cases, they've never met one another—and they all think they're owed money by the company.

Your money, if you're a stockholder.

As an investor, and even as a trader, you have to ask about any company: *Who's* running it? *What* are they doing exactly? *Why* are they doing it right now? Is it founder-led? Has management invested personally into the story or concept? Are they there for their stock position or for their salary and bonus? There's a world of difference between those two things.

In the small-cap markets, where many people are playing on the speculation side, the directors aren't even remotely committed to the companies. They're often on ten or fifteen different boards, so this is just one of their many initiatives. But for you, it's a big investment and it matters. You've got the T-shirt and you're wearing the hat, but then you see that it's just a hobby for the board. It matters more to you than it does to them.

That's what happened with the solar company. To me, it meant everything. To the CEO, I was just one of many fish on the line. He probably had twenty more.

I had 1.5 million shares, but they did a five-for-one split, and then I only had 300,000 shares. That didn't feel as big. My new cost basis went to $1.25 for a share that was now trading at $0.20. So my half-million dollar investment was worth $60,000 and showed no likelihood of returning to the levels I started at anytime soon.

Worse, by now the CEO's real job was selling me stock, not developing solar solutions. And because I wanted to believe, and I wanted to see them succeed, I kept saying, "Hey, Rick, I just bought more shares."

"Great. You're going to be rewarded." And he'd explain how, one day, I'd get my reward and I'd feel good about myself, because that's what the gambler is looking for: any sort of reassurance.

Of course, that's what all CEOs tell you: that the stock will go back up when people understand how cheap it is. That's what the board is paying them to say. It's like a multilevel marketing business in which the business opportunity supersedes the product. Someone comes to your house to try to sell you Tupperware. Ten minutes into it, they're trying to recruit you as another salesperson; that's more impactful to the sales person than selling you the product.

It's the same in penny stock land. What the company does is secondary to the fact that they're trying to sell a stock, because the stock has to keep going up for them to keep telling the story.

And one out of a thousand actually do what they say they're going to do. The other 999 lead to nothing and waste a lot of time and money doing it.

That's why I tell people that small stocks don't deserve your investment. They deserve your speculation, maybe, but not your investment. It's a rusty pool. There's a possible upside, but there's also the high risk of never seeing that capital again.

WHO IS TELLING THE STORY?

Once I got out of the solar energy stock, the peace of mind was worth every penny of the loss. But it was a big loss and a big blow. I should have gotten out a week after the trade first went against me, but ego, greed, fear, and a big dose of people pleasing led to a monumental waste of time and energy. Strangely enough, that bothered me more than the money: the hundreds of hours I wasted because I held on even after I knew I'd made a mistake.

Junior Markets Are Polluted by Design

The solar promotion was one of 1,600 listings on the TSX Venture Exchange in Canada, which exists because it's one of the only ways to raise risk capital for mediocre ideas that the banks and private investors said no to. If you believe you have the next greatest widget, you're not going to be able to raise money unless you have a public listing that people can speculate on. It's inherently incestuous because it depends on getting the speculators bought into the *story*. And as soon as doubt starts to creep in and stock starts to break down, it usually never recovers.

Then the companies roll back and restructure, and they go from solar to uranium or blockchain or psychedelics.

Junior markets are polluted by design. They go back to the gold rush era when a prospector would buy a property claim and go into town on his horse to sell people shares to raise enough money to exploit the property and find gold. He would promise that everyone would be rich.

Even as a kid, I wondered why a prospector who really found a promising gold claim would want to share it. *Wouldn't he take it for himself? Why let anyone else bankroll the project? Why take on partners if the gold was there in the ground?* I would ask myself.

If it was legitimate, he could go to a bank or get investment privately. It's the same with firms on the junior markets. If they have a good business, they can attract private venture capital. They're on the markets because private money and venture capital doesn't want them. It rejected their story. Often there is nothing more to the "future gold mine" than a poorly put together PowerPoint presentation and a chain-smoking scallywag of a chief executive.

People are everything in these microcap penny stock startups. It's really the people you are investing in, so always keep that mindset. Unless they've drunk their own Kool-Aid, they will never complete the mission they are on. It's imperative that the top leadership is invested, emotionally and financially, and that they are the number one cheerleaders. Because if they aren't, then no one else will be. Take it from my experience and do not invest unless the CEO of the company is 100 percent all in as far as his heart, mind, and money are concerned.

But be aware that this is extremely hard to find. It's why you should avoid 99 percent of penny stocks and their CEO pitches. Let the good ones find you, and keep the watch list about quality not quantity.

Gambling Is Part of the American Dream

Studies show that if someone is about to do a line of cocaine, their brain lights up before it even touches their nostril. This is what's called the vacation phenomenon, where the anticipation is more enjoyable than the event itself, like looking forward all year to taking your family to Mexico, then finding it anticlimactic when you arrive.

The market preys on that anticipatory oxytocin boost by offering the possibility of winning. It's been part of American history since the snake oil salesmen in the 1800s and the confidence tricksters of the 1900s. Gambling was and has always been baked into the American dream. Taking risks is the American way. Being a prospector, homesteader, or rancher was gambling of the highest order. Pioneers went all in on a piece of land with no plan B in the hope that someone else would buy their harvest.

"I'll sell it for more than it cost me to someone else later on." The original greater fool theory.

That's what the markets prey on: human nature. Take lottery

tickets, which are often called the idiot tax, because people still buy them even *knowing* that the possibility of getting zero return on the purchase is 99.9 percent. At least penny stocks give you a 1 percent chance rather than a 0.1 percent chance. That's why every junior exchange from Frankfurt to London has thousands of individual startups driving them. The startups move in waves. Until 2020 it was cannabis for five years, followed by psychedelics. That was followed by ESG, or environment, social, and governance. And then the market will swing back around to rare-earth or precious metals, which were all the rage prior to cannabis taking the spotlight in 2014. This is why almost every cannabis debut was an RTO (reverse takeover) from a mineral exploration shell, and this is why many of the cannabis or psychedelic hopefuls will swing around full circle back to mining exploration companies, be it mineral or crypto, within a year or two.

You can bet your shirt on it.

My romance with solar made me a willing idiot. I wanted to have exposure to doing the right thing; I just chose the wrong widget to do it. I could have bought one of the big solar stocks on the NASDAQ, but I got greedy and invested in a startup. The upside was that it had a $1 to $10 probability, not a $10 to $11 probability. But a pro would have bought a good name at ten bucks or more a share, hoping for 10 percent. Instead, I bought at $1 hoping for $10. I played it like a rookie and came out the same.

Tie your trade to your plan. If you don't do what you want to do, you do what the world around you is pushing you to do. That's when you turn into an involuntary investor.

There's always another sucker every day. It's like the gold prospector selling stakes to raise cash. If someone tells you, "I can make you rich. I just need you to sign here and you can be part of this story," you will want to buy in. It's hardwired into us. We all want to be part of the moon shot. If someone tells you, "I've got a sound investment. We've been making money every quarter for seventeen years with no loss. We've got a great management team and huge advisory," your response is likely to be, "I'm not interested in this boring, safe investment. I want the moon shot—I want a *tenbagger*."

The whole market preys on our desire to hit a moon shot.

It's like when investors appear on those TV shows to get money from the "dragons." If you've got that much faith in your idea, why not take it to the bank? Why not get your friends to invest? Why not remortgage your home if you actually, really believe in it? They don't; otherwise, they would have raised capital the traditional way or self-funded by any means possible.

That's the hard reality and the elephant in the room in the startup world. Much of the time, these storytellers just want to be heard.

Look for founders or CEOs that are all in, companies that are founder-led. If they've put every penny they have toward this venture, I'll gladly follow them because I know that they'll give it their all because, otherwise, they're going down with the ship.

An article came out in the early 2000s showing junior stock performance in Toronto. In plain English, it said that companies with very high insider ownership consistently do well; companies without, don't. Period. And dramatically so. It seems obvious, and it is, so pay attention to insider ownership and look for founder-led organizations. Not companies with shill CEOs installed and controlled by the real, nonreporting owners behind the curtain who threw the shell together and are about to promote it using the shareholders money so they can get out and do it again.

I get pitch decks sent to me every single day for the world's latest and greatest whatever. They're strapped for cash despite having the most *disruptive* technology ever and a new Fortune 500 client. Right. Who is telling the story? Do they have a history of creating and selling unicorn companies? Are they obscenely wealthy? If so, why are they still pitching? And if not, why are you entertaining them? Always be mindful of the source, because if it sounds too good to be true, it is.

The Trend Is Your Friend

The market works in trends. A bull market trends up; a bear market trends down. Investors use trends to make decisions. Sometimes it's possible to ride a trend, but there are times you can be a contrarian, someone who goes against the trend because they see an opportunity where no one else does.

AHEAD OF THE TREND

Sometimes contrarians are ahead of the trend, and sometimes they're just wrong. In March 2020, as the world went into lockdown because of the pandemic, my contrarian view was that stocks would be demolished short term as fear elevated. Earnings would surely drop by the end of the year, and the stock market would turn down. Instead, it was one of the biggest years the stock market ever had as people sat at home in their underwear trading stocks on Robinhood, which made the market roar to the upside (thanks also to the US Fed pumping nonstop stimulus money into the system). I put in a huge bet against the markets in March, a big short, that slowly eroded all year until it went to zero.

Bulls Make Money, Bears Make Money, but Pigs Get Slaughtered

When the market is bullish, go long. When the market is bearish, go short. If you're swimming in the direction of the current, it's going to be a lot easier to get where you want to go. It takes half the effort to get there. Be patient and don't swim against the tide, but remember that every trend eventually changes, so keep a look out for the pivot point.

As a participant in the broader market, you should move with the herd. Use the three big US markets—the Dow Jones, the S&P, and the NASDAQ—as benchmarks. I like to use the analogy of the shooter on the grassy knoll. Once you take your shot, you're going to give away your position, so make sure you've got the shot before you take it. Get confirmation and make sure you're seeing what you're looking for in the trends. And be professional with your expectations. Remember: the amateur comes into the market with $10,000 hoping to make $100,000. The professional brings in $100,000 and hopes to make $10,000. Which one has to work harder? Which one has the stats in their favor? And which one can do this consistently day in and day out? The pro.

You don't have to be brilliant or lucky to win in the market. You don't have to find something clever or obscure. If you only need to make 10 percent, you don't have to reinvent the wheel.

"Everyone's an expert in a bull market," the saying goes. When the market's going up every day, everyone feels like they know what they're doing. That's when one needs to be most careful, because it's too easy to get a false sense that it's easy when things are going good, when in fact all you need to do is be *in* the market to make a profit. Be cognizant of price appreciation based on just being there versus actually making a decision or a directional call. It's like real estate: oftentimes, you simply need to be in the market to make money on paper. That doesn't mean you are skilled or that you specifically timed it. You were simply present during that period.

Taking the Lead to Win

The history of business is full of outstanding gamblers who ignored the haters because they spotted a pivot point, an opportunity. The V-8 engine, which solidified Ford's dominance, almost lost Henry Ford all his investors. People said he couldn't put eight cylinders in a single block of steel. Ford put his five top engineers in a room and told them, "Don't come out until you have a V-8." They came up with something no one in the world had even imagined in 1928: an opposing eight-cylinder engine block cast from a single piece of steel, making it mass-producible and affordable for most people.

Ford bet his entire life and reputation on the V-8 engine block, and that bet *built* the Ford Motor Company.

In 2004, I got my medical cannabis license because I knew the industry was about to take off. Everybody thought I was crazy to believe cannabis would become an industry, but I knew—and I was right. It just turned out I was a decade early. It took about twelve years to turn on formally, when Sanjay Gupta appeared on CNN in 2013 and said, "I was wrong," (about cannabis having some known medical benefits) and introduced this rapidly expanding sector to the masses on prime-time. I started investing in 2004, and no one else showed up until around 2014. When the public got out of bed on the space in 2018, the whole sector blew up after a decade-plus run. In typical fashion, it sold off once the masses arrived at the party.

I waited a long time, but I never lost conviction. No one else agreed with me, but it didn't matter. It was like the story of the V-8 engine. If you believe something will work, it doesn't matter if it doesn't exist yet. You can get in early, assuming you have the time to wait.

Getting ahead of the trend can be difficult because so many forces are trying to influence your thinking. It's important to understand why. Stock market news and news services exist to advertise, like a local newspaper with a single story—the "news hole" as it's called in the biz—in the middle of a page completely surrounded by advertisements. The "news" they peddle is often paid-for advertising, and even if it's not, it's guaranteed to be in line with the interests of the advertisers who pay the editors' wages. In short, commercial news, unto itself, is an inherent conflict of interest. It's not news at all; it's all opinion—bought and paid for.

The same corporate influence and manipulation happens all the time in the stock market as well as in Hollywood, local and federal government, and in professional sports. The largest advertiser in the NFL for example is Anheuser-Busch, the brewing giant, which clearly feels very threatened by the potential legalization of cannabis in America. Even if legal weed takes just 1 percent of their top line over the next ten years, that's simply not acceptable to them, not with the money they pay lawmakers and advertisers to shape how to make Americans think about beer. Anheuser-Busch makes it part of its sponsorship that NFL players are not permitted to use or openly discuss cannabis. Anheuser-Busch has made it clear to the NFL that if a cannabis company were to ever put an ad in the Super Bowl, they will pull their NFL budget. The NFL heavily relies on the more than $250 million they receive from Anheuser-Busch each year, so it's handcuffed to what the beer giant will or will not permit it to do. In Calgary, Alberta, at the annual Stampede, aka "The Greatest Outdoor Show on Earth," there can't be any cannabis advertising within a kilometer because the beer industry is so afraid of the competition. Guess who made the rule? Anheuser-Busch. Guess who owns the beer garden contracts? Guess who has a lot to lose financially if cannabis use were permitted as well? So what do they do? They create unethical and illegal rules in a country that has already legalized cannabis.

If you're the most bullish guy in cannabis in North America, and yet the NFL and the Calgary Stampede have outlawed your product, you're a long way ahead of the curve. Maybe too far. You'll be all on your own until sentiment begins to shift on a macro level. You can wait on those MSOS ETF call options for a little while longer.

Unreliable Information from Conflicted Sources

The line between news and advertising is blurred everywhere when it comes to the stock market. At the top of the food chain, CNBC proudly calls itself "First in business worldwide," but it takes advertising money from public companies every single day. Guess who owns CNBC? NBC. Guess who owns NBC? Comcast. Who owns Comcast you ask? Naturally it's Vanguard and BlackRock, with a combined ownership of 705 million shares of Comcast.

The primary business of Vanguard and BlackRock is to sell you, the public, shares of their portfolio companies and or shares in their in-house ETFs that buy their portfolio companies with your money. How do they do that? They get plastic-faced talking heads on CNBC to declare absurd things and host doe-eyed guests who will say exactly what they're there to say—nothing more, nothing less. "First in business worldwide." CNBC is about as factual with economics and companies as CNN is with stats and politics. It's a rag, a propaganda outlet, and a megaphone for their domestic and international clients.

CNBC will introduce a CEO—"We've got Lisa Su from AMD"— to tell you how great an opportunity it is for the stock right now, but it doesn't put up a disclaimer that AMD has paid for the four-minute segment, nor that its primary shareholders are Vanguard and BlackRock, CNBC's mommy and daddy. It's a blatant conflict of interest, but the stock volume goes up, and everyone is happy.

At the bottom of the food chain, micro-cap companies release misleading "tout sheets," and penny stock criminals use private blogs to plug, say, the next greatest battery technology, claiming that it's going to be inevitably bought up by Tesla Motors. They drop the Tesla name in the article both as clickbait and as SEO juice to attract eyeballs (impressions, which in turn sell the ad space) that come from "Tesla" searches for the following days and weeks.

You are the eyeballs; *you* are the product. The very fact that you tuned to the channel becomes a viewer statistic. The media outlet then goes and sells those metrics to a sponsoring company. In the micro-cap world, there's a swath of marketing companies that employ armies of outstanding spin-doctor writers with no other job than to come up with a $50,000–$250,000 story for a startup. The writers use tricks like incorporating the name of an established business in the field to create clickbait—like Tesla—so that their articles get picked up by Google searches that would miss them otherwise.

Be hypervigilant and aware of these scams. One or two guys have created a company and are now locked and loaded, waiting to blast their shares into the unexpecting public. They spend their shareholder money on promoting the stock, and then as soon as it rises, they sell their shares, often illegally, offshore or in other people's names. It's a smash-and-grab in broad daylight. When you see a public company featured heavily in the "news," it often means there are large sellers ready with their fingers on the triggers, and you're the bait to create the liquidity they're waiting for. You're the *greater fool* money that has to come in so the smart (early) money can get out.

In the crypto world, this is even worse. With the float of most of the hyped-up coins being held within only a small handful of anonymous wallets. If it's being pumped, rest assured, there are con men dumping into the incoming volume.

Typically, the smarter money you are, the bigger money you are, the earlier you get in, and the earlier you get out. When a stock or coin is being promoted, whether a big or small company, there's usually a temporary reason for it.

Next time you see a banner on your newsfeed or on Yahoo Finance boasting, "These two stocks are the ones to watch," look for the tiny disclaimer at the bottom telling you what media company got the kicker to manufacture this shite article and broadly disseminate it during market hours. Learn about the shady world of "check swaps" and how issuers and promoters deal out free stock in creative ways so as to not show up as compensation. Oftentimes when you are reading an investor article about a stock, you are really reading a compensated piece, leg-humping the company that gave that writer stock in a way that does not need to be disclosed.

Your Information Is as Good as It Costs

I buy information. I subscribe to several independent newsletters by various specialists who track and report on particular areas of investment, such as resources, tech, or energy. Around $100 a year can get you some reliable information because it allows the specialists to be completely independent and work for their subscriber group, not the companies they talk about—a significant difference. A lot of them used to work in the banks or trading floors, and they saw how corrupt it all was and started working for themselves in an effort to help the little guy. They never drop "hot" tickers; they never boost emotions. They simply report facts. The same with money managers who report, "Our portfolio has been steadily accumulating X, Y, or Z stock since the last third quarter." They're usually trying to educate, not manipulate.

It's a far cry from the kind of stock tips they had in the movie *Wall Street*: "Blue Horseshoe loves Anacott Steel."

There are also expert market traders who have made a tremendous name for themselves doing nothing but shorting into "hot tips" and stock calls from certain "experts." They know the game, and they are calling the bluffs and shorting into the paid pumps. It can be a profitable vocation if you know how to execute.

The general rule with tips in the markets remains what Lao Tzu wrote 2,400 years ago: "Those who know, do not speak. Those who speak, do not know."

KNOW WHERE YOU ARE

When you've been an investor or trader for any length of time, you'll know there are constantly new things that influence the flow of capital in the market: a trade war, anything to do with petroleum, any political events, bond yields, interest rates. There's a ten-day news cycle, and good traders need to know when to leverage this noise and when to mute it.

It's all about discipline and knowing where we are in the broader picture. Are we in an Iran–Israel conflict? Did the Democrats just win the US presidency?

Be Where the Puck Is Going to Be

If an investor knows where the markets are in that overall macro trend, they can avoid whipsawing back and forth based on the daily movements, which is a recipe for frustration and loss. You're always reacting when you should be following the recipe. You're chasing the play when you should be ahead of it.

As the ice hockey great Wayne Gretzky put it, "You want to be where the puck is going to be." The only way to do that is to put on the blinders, stay in your lane, and go with your gut. Don't react to every single news story. Get properly educated and experienced, and then use your intuition as all good traders do.

The best reason for following your intuition is that you only have yourself to blame. There's not much worse knowing that you knew better and did it anyway. A bad business decision is no different from "I know I shouldn't have this cigarette, but I'm going to have it anyway." It sounds and looks stupid.

At least if you stick to your plan and something unforeseen happens, you did the best you could.

It goes back to understanding that there is an energy and a trend. And if you're going to buck the trend, you're about to do a

U-turn in traffic. And if you get into a head-on collision, it's not their fault; it's your fault.

A Strong Sense of Intuition

The very best traders in the world have a strong sense of intuition and listen to their gut. They're usually right because they know what to listen to. Take Ray Dalio and Warren Buffett. As mentioned earlier, they seem to have a crystal-ball-like intuition, where they are completely convinced that they're right. If they're overexposed to something, they distribute any excess or unbalanced positions back into the market to increase liquidity so that they can act when the next buying opportunity arises.

Every investor needs the same kind of strong internal rudder. You need to know you're making the right call. If you don't feel it, don't do anything. There has to be some conviction in your belly for putting money on the line, if for no other reason than it makes it easier to sleep at night.

Doing nothing is fine. For most people, however, the temptation to act is almost too much. Few people can open up their brokerage account and then just sit there. They want to *do* something. They want to move something. They're going to buy, sell, hold, buy, sell, hold. Because every day of a trader's life brings the same three options: buy, sell, hold.

You have to find a way to discipline yourself. I keep a sign by my desk that says in giant bold letters, "Cash is a position." Even if you're dying to deploy some, lift your finger off the trigger. You can say to yourself, "I've got my X amount of cash. That's a position! I don't need to take a stock position today because having cash grants me the ability to make more decisions tomorrow."

Cash is a position. That's a very powerful sentence in this business.

I often open up my accounts in the morning, and even if I have limited time, I start to think about a trade. If I hadn't opened my computer, I'd be just fine because my positions are good: out of sight out of mind. But because I'm looking at it, I feel inclined to start tinkering, to add a little of this or trim a little of that. Being attention deficit and unable to sit tight in business and in life is very dangerous; in trading it's sure death.

Trading Is Not Binary

Constant news is very bad for traders because it fuels their attention-deprived brain and whips them back and forth on emotion. Traders need to inhabit the gray area between the extremes. To think like a professional, traders have to understand that trading is not a binary game of buying stocks, then selling them. There is no black and white in life, only shades of gray—and that's *especially* true in stock trading.

Professional traders and investors *accumulate* their positions over time, sometimes years, before they reach some turning point or catalyst when they flip the switch to distribution mode and start to sell that position back into the market. I cannot stress this enough. Expert equity traders simply do not buy and sell everything in one go. Instead, they buy in tranches over time—sometimes hours, sometimes months—and then, when ready, they distribute shares back into the market, also over a period of time, selling the position back in intervals.

I can't begin to count how much money I've lost from not doing this properly and how well I've done when I accumulate and distribute more gradually and patiently. Trading is as much about patience as it is about execution.

Investing in any type of trading financial instruments is far from a black and white, buy and sell game. It's only when one realizes this that one can become a professional. Every day, I hear investors say, "I sold way too soon," or "I bought way too much and should have waited." But the timing isn't their mistake. Their mistake is their *entire* approach. Their whole system is flawed.

It makes far more sense to scale into a position rather than buy it all at once. To buy $100,000 worth of stock, you should only be buying $15,000–$20,000 at a time. If you buy it all at once, you're just playing blackjack. It's reckless for your portfolio, and it will fuck up your mind. If you get a big gap-down the day after you bought, you'll be feeling stuck or vulnerable, with few options. This is even truer if you are buying or trading on margin.

Say you start buying ABC stock in January at one-tenth of the position at $10 a share, and then buy the rest over a period of weeks. You're not only protecting and preserving your capital in case something goes wrong, like a big market crash; you're also able to take advantage of dips in the price. That will help you with dollar-cost averaging. So when the stock rolls over at $20 and starts to come back down, you can start to offer up that position in, say, one-fifths while still keeping your core position in place in case it starts to go back up again.

It's even more important to sell over time than it is to buy over time. No serious investor in the world—no mutual fund, no hedge fund, no trader—is ever in and out in one go.

Use the market as it's intended. Step in and out quietly. Try not to clunk in and out, making a big racket. Remember that stealth is wealth and that finesse is almost as important as timing.

People who want to go all in risk being underwater overnight. Instead of asking themselves every day whether they should buy, sell, or hold, they should instead be thinking, "I'm in accumulation mode, so I'm going to buy a little," or "I'm in distribution mode, so I'll just sell a little into today's move."

Now you have a business that you're actually *treating like a business*, which is when you start to make money. Go back and read the manual. Go back and refer to your journal. What are you doing? Are you accumulating or distributing? Are you moving away from your tech holdings and toward commodities? The answers shouldn't change today or tomorrow morning.

This approach is a far cry from the impression the media creates of a black-and-white environment of buy, sell, or hold. The question doesn't actually apply to those of us already on a mission. The Jim Cramers of the world exist purely to distract the people who have no plan! It's true that there are technical traders who react every day to news or microtrends and swing in and out in a minute, but they're specialists and that is their niche. Their job is to be reactive and high frequency. You may want that life, but I can tell you, it's not for most people.

If a position doesn't feel good, I often find myself selling out half of it and then assessing. If it still doesn't feel great, I will continue until I've sold it all. If you don't know what to do, and you're not sure about your accumulation/distribution program, reducing your exposure by 50 percent keeps you in the gray. You still have your upside exposure, but you've also reduced your risk by half. If the holding goes down tomorrow, you've now got cash to take advantage of that dip and add a bit more if you're dying to stay in the position. If the trade goes against your plan, you can start the process of redistribution back into the market.

If you've got a $100,000 position that looks very good, you might think, "Should I double it?" No. You should add another $10,000, so 10 percent or so, and wait for your confirmation signals before you add the next 10 or 20 percent.

Always stick with the general trend of being a net buyer or net seller, and don't take singular actions. It's a process, not a moment.

People hear this and say to me, "Holy shit. I've never even thought about it like that."

I tell them, "Yes. That's why you lose money every month and call me and say, 'What am I doing wrong?'"

When Carl Icahn sold the last of his Herbalife shares in mid-2021, which was a $400 million position, he did it over hundreds of days. He started buying it in 2013 and made over $1.3 billion in total on the trade. What does that indicate about scaling in and scaling out over time?

The Market Is Smarter than You, Whether It's Drunk or Sober

In 2020 the market kept rising regardless of the pandemic and the lockdown. I blew myself up trying to short the market before I gave up, but the market just continued to irrationally go higher. You can have all the reasons in the world why you're right, but the market doesn't care. Don't buck the major trends. When the market doesn't do what you predicted, remember the brilliant warning of the economist John Maynard Keynes: "The stock market can remain irrational longer than you can remain solvent."

Remember this on your next big-short trade idea.

I've seen it before, and I've been burned before. After Lehman Brothers crashed in September 2008, March 2009 was the bottom of the market. Ford, as one example, was over $5 at the beginning of 2008, it fell to about $1.15 in February of 2009, and then was up six or seven times that again by the end of 2009. It was a dramatic pivot. The market went back up at a time when I and others thought there was still a lot more bleeding to come. We weren't in the market, and we missed a fortune because the market corrected itself and decided that everything was rosy a mere couple of months after the financial crisis. The underlying issues that had caused the Bear Stearns and Lehman Brothers bankruptcies had not been solved, but the market drank the Kool-Aid of a perfect V-shaped recovery and took off anyway. No one wanted to ask the hard questions; they wanted it all in the rearview.

You can be highly intelligent or you can be an idiot, but the market doesn't care. If that broader trend is rolling, there's no bucking it. It's going to go whether or not it's supposed to.

Focus on
Asset Preservation

No one needs to go into the stock markets to generate wealth. When I started out, I could have chosen to parlay my cash into land or housing or other permanent assets. I could have locked it away to guarantee not just my future and my wife's but my kids' too. I could have chosen almost anything. Instead, I scratched an itch. I became an independent market speculator.

It was a compulsive choice, like all gambling. When a gambler wins at the racetrack, he doesn't usually go back to his car. Instead he goes right back to the ticket window and places another bet because he's feeling hot. And he carries on until the day ends or until he's lost everything he won.

It's a compulsion. Compulsion is how bookmakers win. It's how casinos win. It's how the stock market wins. And it's how people like me—and people like *you*—can lose if we aren't focused on return of capital.

RETURN *OF* CAPITAL, NOT RETURN *ON* CAPITAL

I remind myself every day that keeping what you have is way more important than trying to make more.

If you have a million dollars, make more of a priority of preserving it than of trying to grow it, because as long as you have it, you have options. Say you use it to buy a house. Well, your new home comes with a $1,000-per-month landscaping bill, but you don't have a $12,000 per year budget to keep your yard pretty. It also has a $15,000 per year property tax bill and $15,000 per year electricity bill. Another $30,000 you hadn't budgeted. What seemed like a sound investment has ended up jeopardizing your money and chipping away at your net worth. I was told as a kid that any fool can get lucky and make a million bucks by winning the lottery or hitting it big on a stock, but that the real test is turning it into two or three million. In fact, I realize now that the *really* hard part is still having that original million two or three years later. There are land mines, paywalls, and tempting things to buy at every turn. It takes tremendous discipline and willpower to preserve capital.

Don't Neglect Your Assets

Everyone has assets, the things that add value to their lives. It's the things you own, of course, but it's also your spouse or your family, your health and your time, and your ability to do math in your head or to hang drywall. Everyone avoids making bad decisions about those kinds of assets. They don't neglect their possessions, they don't cheat on their spouse or mistreat their children, and they don't lose the tools that enable them to make money.

Why be any more careless with your capital? It's way more important not to lose it than to increase it. If you can, it's better to wait all year for the right trade to come along rather than rushing in when you're not ready. Holding on to your capital, focusing on the return *of* it as much as the return *on* it, is your equivalent of a sniper waiting patiently for the right shot. And it's fucking hard. Think it's hard being in a casino with $500 burning a hole in your pocket? Try watching CNBC with your brokerage account open in front of you and $1 million cash at the ready.

That's discipline. That's having a plan and knowing when to take the shot.

Money Is One of the Energies of Life. Be a Good Host to It

If an investor finds themselves with $5,000, the key is to allocate it carefully: $1,000 here, $1,000 there, and maybe $3,000 in a money market account. Your $5,000 is "gone," but you're holding a great hand. Once you're a good host to money, you can start to attract more money.

One of the first financial books I read talked about the importance of "paying yourself first." In *The Automatic Millionaire* (2003), David Bach talks about "the latte factor," the way in which regular small payments, like $5 for a latte, amount up to more than we give credit for over time, especially compared to the possible return if the same money were invested. It's $1,825 a year for your double-pump nonfat soy latte habit. Over a career of, say, twenty-five years at a modest 5 percent annual interest rate, that's $100,000. Say you have four or five other daily factors like that. Even at only $5, that's another $500,000. A $40 lunch per day is $680,000 over twenty-five years.

You can spend that money on something that doesn't matter that much to you, or you could use it for something you really want. You could buy an early retirement plan. How many lattes taste that good?

By Enriching Your Life Every Day, You're Buying Yourself That Day

When you're allocating your assets, don't forget yourself. Pay yourself first. When I get a $5,000 check, the first thing I do is put $2,000 into something I know I will see again. Whatever happens, 40 percent of that money will be preserved.

If you get a check for $10,000, force yourself to put $4,000 into an investment or bank where it won't disappear on you. You're investing it in yourself for something that gives you joy: retirement, a trip, sports gear, art supplies . . . whatever you're into. Most people get the check, pay their taxes, pay their rent, buy some food and clothing, and then they've got a minimal amount to get them to the next check. To make ends meet.

That's not living; it's a trap. You work so hard, and you pay everyone else but forget to pay yourself?

It's Not about Money; It's about Runway

All the cash assets you force yourself to put away go toward your runway. If I need $100,000 a year to live, and I find myself with $50,000 of savings, I have bought myself six months of my life. At any time, I can decide to go on a sabbatical for six months. If I reach $200,000 of savings, I have a two-year runway available to me.

Once you have a two-year runway locked and loaded in the bank, for all intents and purposes, you're financially independent. Now you have the ability to start to make some investments, start a business, go on vacation—even to write a book. Once you create a runway for yourself, the choice is yours. You're not trying to hoard dollars. You're trying to use the energy in those dollars to buy choices, options, time, freedom. Paying yourself first is a critical habit on the journey to financial independence.

Find a Fee-Based Advisor

Wealthy investors pay experts to give them their opinion and nothing more. The rest of us rely on bank employees whose job is to sell us something. That's a life-changing advantage for people with money.

Virtually every advisor who works on commission or for a bank has an inherent conflict of interest. The advisor telling you to buy TD Bank mutual funds is sitting in a TD Bank office wearing a TD Bank name tag and collecting a TD Bank paycheck thanks to your investments that he clips a fee on. Instead, you can find a professional and proven independent financial advisor who won't try to sell you anything because he doesn't have anything to sell. It may cost you $1,000 an hour, because objectivity doesn't come cheap. For that, he'll look objectively at your situation and give you the best advice he can for an hour. That can be invaluable to you long-term. That one hour can change the course of your life for the better, as I have experienced each time I have sought out unbiased advice from a professional.

It's All about Risk

For millennia, higher risks have brought higher returns. That's why a good advisor will ask you right off the bat, "What is your risk tolerance?" They'll ask about your comfort levels: your net worth, your experience in the market, what you will do if something goes wrong. They'll want to understand whether you might need money for emergencies. Are you a gung-ho person or a fearful person? If they don't ask you those questions, fire them immediately. Find another who wants to understand the whole picture before he makes any suggestions.

Preserve Your Castle

Your time is valuable. The time you spend trading is doubly so. Put rules in place to protect it. My devices are all set up to give me *zero* notifications, and I never answer the phone when it rings. If Bob calls and you haven't spoken to him in a long time, it's going to be a forty-five-minute catch-up. If it's in the middle of your day, it might cost you at a time when you can't afford the forty-five minutes. Maybe you'll miss exiting a position at the market close on a Friday, and suddenly you've got a position in your mind all weekend because you took an unexpected call on Bob's terms, and Bob made you a longer-term holder than you planned.

That makes it a very expensive catch-up. And it happens to people all the time.

If you check your emails when you get up and someone has a query, you can choose to answer it. Ten minutes later, they reply with another question, and you reply again. An hour later, you've had five or six exchanges, but the issue is still going on at 11:00 a.m. A half hour later, you finally speak on the phone and sort it out. But you didn't get to go for your run or do everything you needed to do in the morning. Instead, if you ignore the first email, do all your important things, and finally check it at 11:00 a.m., you'll often find that the issue has already been sorted out. Don't react immediately to other people if you don't have to. Their problem is not your problem.

THE BANKING SCAM

The banking system is designed to turn independent investors into fee-generating machines. Every bank on the planet charges monthly fees because they build their cash-flow models based on getting $5–$10 a month in fees from each account holder. Then they give you a credit card, which costs you $200 a year in fees. Then they give you a mortgage, which brings them $30,000 a year in interest payments, and maybe a loan, which gives them another $12,000 a year in interest. All of which comes from you, Mr. or Mrs. Valued Customer.

The bank will get you to meet with a "qualified investment advisor," aka a mutual fund salesperson. In the United States or Canada, that means someone who has taken a one-day mutual fund sales training course. One day. It takes five times longer to learn how to operate a forklift or get your Level 1 First Aid certification. When you visit the bank to talk to Debbie, the nice lady who tells you what to do with your retirement statements, bear in mind that just six months ago, Debbie was likely a teller behind the counter handling deposits and withdrawals like a human ATM. Before that, she might have come from the fast-food industry. It's not her fault, but she's not qualified to give anyone financial advice, especially in return for commissions being pulled right out of your retirement account.

The mutual fund sales course in Canada is less than a weekend. Mutual fund sales people can get both their professional qualification and a life-insurance license by passing one written test after reading a single textbook. That enables them to make major economic and life decisions for you and your family. They have less education in the markets than you can give yourself in a couple of days with a few good books. They get paid whether or not you make money through a scheme called management expense ratios, or MERs. If you walk into a bank with $100,000, Debbie will put it into a balanced portfolio run by a money manager in New York and charge you about 2 percent a year for the luxury of being in an underperforming bank-managed fund.

That's $2,000 for the pleasure of working with Debbie, the financial savant, on something you could easily do yourself at home. It's a racket. If your portfolio drops to $90,000, you still give $2,000 to the bank. If you make money, the first $2,000 goes to the bank. If you factor in the $2,000 over ten or fifteen years, a big portion of your gains and your capital are eroded by letting a retail bank take advantage of you.

Don't Give Your Money to the Bank; Buy the Bank

Alternatively, you could leave your big-box retail bank, join a local credit union, and hire a fee-based financial advisor. You remove the bias and get real advice, and the credit union and financial advisor don't have their hands in your pockets. The financial world is so competitive that there are many free ways to park, invest, or move money.

Traditionally, people turned to gold as bank insurance, or as a hedge against inflation. It was a way to park some "emergency" money outside of the system, either in your own hands or secured somewhere. If banks close down again or if there is a prolonged power outage, there is no way to get physical money from the banks or ATMs, so holding some cash and some gold in a safe place is never a bad idea. Today, some people use crypto in the same way—though bear in mind that decentralized finance (DeFi) is still in its very early days, and risks still outweigh potential gains if you don't fully understand the DeFi ecosystem.

As for cash, it is a useful balance against exposure elsewhere, but the paper fiat money in your wallet or in your bank account is not quite as secure as it might seem. Traditionally, *money* has seven characteristics:

- ▸ *Acceptability:* People recognize it as a medium of exchange, and it has the same value to everyone.
- ▸ *Divisibility:* It can be used to pay in high or low amounts easily.
- ▸ *Portability:* It is easy to transport, carry, and hold on your person. Small enough to do day-to-day commerce easily.
- ▸ *Recognizability:* It is immediately identifiable and recognized by all with a standardized value.
- ▸ *Homogeneity:* Each unit is identical to all the others.
- ▸ *Durability:* It does not deteriorate with use or time.
- ▸ *Scarcity:* It is not abundant throughout the country or system. Large amounts of it would be rare and its supply tightly protected.

If you think about it, paper fiat money is no longer scarce at all, and it's widely recognized as a losing asset. On Wall Street, traders refer to stock market gains as opposed to return on cash investments as "Cash is trash." Both Bitcoin and gold fit those seven characteristics better than government-issued paper money, even though gold is not as portable as Bitcoin. Many economists consider paper money to be debt, not money, as it is a treasury note held against a government that is largely indebted.

As a rule, though, most of us are still paying banks to take our paper money and hold it. Instead, do what bankers do: buy and own shares in the bank. Every year, the bank makes money, and its stock price goes higher while it exploits you and your cash using *fractional reserve banking*. It takes your $100 and lends $1,200 to the next customer; it is by very definition a Ponzi scheme.

The difference between being an owner and being a wage slave in a vast Ponzi scheme of government-issued debt is equity, or ownership. Some people don't want equity; they just want their pay every month...and that's fine. But others see it differently: they want to be in the owners' box. They want to be on the right side of the table and act like an institution by becoming an autonomous investor. They think things like, "I'll forgo my monthly stipend for 5 percent of the whole business."

Once they do that, they can see how equity is the ultimate game changer. It means they get to own the types of assets directly that the bank is trying to sell them all bundled up in their overpriced mutual funds and ETFs. This can include debt, bank equities, preferred shares, precious metals, commercial real estate, and maybe a little Bitcoin or Ethereum.

Most importantly, if you are planning to have lots of money and want money to stick around and multiply for you, ensure you educate yourself intimately on each asset that you want to own. Become a subject-matter expert on it. This is key to feeling good about your investments. As crypto starts to overtake gold as the de facto hedge against fiat currency devaluation, be aware of the risks and study DeFi like a student would at a university. Situations like Mt. Gox—the Japanese crypto exchange that went bust in 2014 after its holdings disappeared, likely stolen—are still possible. Linchpins—single points of failure—very much exist in crypto. It is still very, very early, and early tech is always superseded as we learn from our mistakes.

Put another way, when Napster crippled the music industry with free MP3s in 1999 and then Apple sealed the deal with the iPod in 2001, CDs—the physical competitor—died as a result. They didn't actually lose all their value, they just became a clunky, secondary option. But people didn't throw them out, because the music on the disc still held value to them.

As long as people want to own Bitcoin or to own and wear gold, Bitcoin and gold will both have value in their respective arenas at the opposite end of the digital-to-analog spectrum. An MP3 is only $0.99, yet there is still a market for a $20 vinyl record of the same track. Things are only worth what other people are willing to pay for them, and that swings back and forth like an ocean tide over years and decades.

The world of non-fungible tokens (NFTs)—online things that can't be replaced by something similar—is changing everything, but no one knows the future impact. It might be a mere fad, or it might be as permanently disruptive to money as MP3s were to music. Different people give very different answers. Some say the mania for NFTs is just like it was for Beanie Babies, internet stocks, or tulips in seventeenth-century Holland. Others say that Web3 and NFTs won't or can't experience the same initial bust that the internet experienced in 2000, because demand will only go up. But eventually, gravity always kicks in; the only question is to what extent and what will it look like after the initial pullback from this parabolic entry to the world.

Watch It Disappear

When my son was born in September of 2008, I took the nest egg I'd been saving since I started working—my first $40,000—and I gave it to a commissioned mutual fund salesperson. I figured he could put it to work in the market. The salesperson worked on a commission of about 2 percent, which would have gotten him $800, and that's not enough even for him to remember my name. So he got me to use my money to leverage it against a loan, to borrow against it like a mortgage, which turned that $40,000 into $160,000 by way of a $120,000 loan, also known as 4-for-1 leverage, through another predatory institution called AGF.

Great for the "investment advisor." Now he was into a $3,200 commission off the bat, so that's at least enough to get his attention. But I was investing $160,000, which turned into only $80,000 a few months later in the September 2008 crash. Not only had I lost my $40,000; I also owed AGF Financial another $40,000 of margin debt.

The professional advisor had made my $40,000 worth *negative* $40,000 in only a few months.

This kind of horror story happens every day. In 2010 there was an investor in Seattle who started with $10,000 in his full service stock brokerage account, and a couple of years later, he owed his broker over $1 million due to too much leverage and bad bets. This and my case are extreme examples of something all too common in the investment brokerage world.

My trusted mutual fund salesman completely fucked me, and possibly many others, by using leverage where it was reckless and self-seeking to do so. If your broker or advisor recommends leverage, ask them to simulate what would happen to the account if we had another Lehman Brothers scenario.

When the 2008 collapse came along, everyone who was leveraged was badly hurt. That's what caused the whole thing, leverage. I blame my compulsive trigger finger. I had $40,000 burning a hole in my bank account, so I was determined to do something "smart" with it. But I only thought of what it could earn me, not what I could potentially lose. Something like a guaranteed investment certificate in Canada, or even a money market account, makes it 99 percent certain I'd see that money again. When you invest, ask yourself, "What's more important? Return *on* this capital or return *of* this capital?" How much can you afford to ultimately lose in the pursuit of those juicy gains?

On the penny stock markets, where many independent investors lose money every day, nine out of ten ventures eventually go bust or restructure within three years. The law of averages says that if you put $40,000 into a startup, there's about a 90 percent probability you won't see it again. The startup has a far greater probability of closing shop than it does of providing you a return on investment. Never forget this. Or better yet, wait for that clean kill, and do it with capital you can afford to lose.

Also, avoid mutual fund salespeople and penny stock pirates like you would any other charlatan who was after your nest egg.

COUCH POTATO INVESTING

Debbie at the bank doesn't lose if you lose; the bank wins every single year, regardless. If you go to your bank with $100,000 to invest, they'll give you a cup of coffee and tell you about three popular boilerplate portfolios: an *aggressive* one with a high rate of return but more volatility and risk; a *medium-risk* one, where you can expect fairly reasonable conservative gains and moderate risk; and a *conservative* portfolio with virtually no return but virtually no risk of loss. That's the three-point system the retail investment world is built on. Although they pretend that it's tailor-made for you, it's the exact opposite. The system is set up to keep you at an average return around 5–10 percent a year, thanks mostly to cash-based investments in the basket that effectively lose you money every year due to inflation. These investments also grossly under-perform the stock indexes every single year.

Considering they have high-paid portfolio managers running the funds, that's utterly unacceptable and opportunistic. It's an embarrassment to the entire industry that pretends nothing is wrong with the 1950s system of templated fund sales.

Index funds that match the Dow Jones or S&P 500 yield about 11 percent per year on average, going back over fifty years, but they can be highly volatile and subject to flash crashes and economic downturns. Balanced funds are usually around 5 percent a year, with less dramatic swings in value, which suits most retired people. Money-market funds—the low-risk type, which include bonds, T-bills, and cash equivalents—won't lose anything even if the market crashes, but they won't go up either. They're also subject to the increasing fiat money supply diluting your buying power due to rising inflation.

That is the investment world for the masses. There are only three options, none of them are great, and all three have been the go-to since the very first days of the automobile.

They Don't Believe in Their Own Product

About 85 percent of money managers in the world underperform the stock market every single year. And every single year, the combined fees they earn for missing the mark add up to many billions of dollars. Over a century, the S&P has netted out an average of about 11 percent, while the average mutual fund has netted 4 percent. So you pay a mutual fund manager 2 or 3 percent to underperform the market by half.

You pay them to lose your money.

What's worse, less than 1 percent of mutual fund managers have a single dollar in their own fund. They don't believe in their own product. They know the game, and they don't want to get retailed when they can buy wholesale index funds or go right to shares in the bank or institution.

They suggest they're going to "manage" your money, which is an appealing idea, but in reality, you're paying them to underperform the market potentially with your life savings, with everything you've got, as was my case in 2008. You're doing that because you haven't educated yourself. You haven't read the books. You don't realize that cash is a position and that cash also affords you choices. There should be no rush when it comes to picking investments.

If you want to find out more about this, read *A Little Book of Common Sense Investing: The Only Way to Guarantee Your Fair Share of Stock Market Returns* (2007) by John C. Bogle, the godfather of the index fund. Be warned: it will make you feel a little nauseous to realize how you're being ripped off. But you'll feel empowered, too, because there are some easy changes you can make right away.

The Dark Secret of the Money Management Industry

The answer for passive investors is called index investing, or couch-potato investing. The couch potato strategy is based on the contrasting hundred-year performance of the S&P and mutual funds: 11 percent versus 5 percent. Why not just put your money into the index? You'll do less work and pay lower fees to get a higher return. Why would anyone hire an active manager if they can't even beat the index? If you put $100,000 into the S&P 500 and didn't even look at it, apart from taking about five minutes per year to rebalance it, you'd outperform most of the top-paid money managers on the planet.

Stockbrokers are an essential piece of the markets, yes, but really just to take buy-and-sell orders for people who don't want to do it online. They are often called investment advisors, though none of them has ever given me a single piece of investment advice. All they do is make the trade when I say, "Can you buy me five hundred shares of Suncor at twenty dollars?" They've been made redundant by digital computing and online brokerages, yet they still make fortunes—typically $100 each time you place a trade. The online brokerage firms usually charge about $5 per trade. Having access to a good stockbroker can be make or break for certain penny-stock investors that might need rumors or hearsay "from the street," but the full-service broker model is slowly dying out. More and more independents are turning to the discount brokerage world and taking control of their own trading.

There are two ways to make a trade. If you have $100 to spare, you can make a call, hope your broker answers, listen to him chewing his lunch, and ask him to buy one hundred shares of something. He may or may not give you his opinion for three or four minutes, which will be amateur at best, then you wait for him to say, "Okay, you own it." Alternatively, you could open an online broker app on your cell phone or computer and enter in the stock, get a real-time quote on the price, enter "500 shares" and your limit price, and click confirm. It asks if you're sure, and then whammo, you bought the shares for five bucks in fifteen seconds with no human interference.

To deal with a human broker who might know less about finance than your brother-in-law or your neighbor, you have to pay 95 percent more than you need to. Most brokers want to help, and they do try their best, but at the end of the day, they are clipping your money whether or not they succeed. The model is inherently flawed: the broker has no capital at risk and they get paid. You put up all the capital and take all the risks, and you get paid after them.

It's the opposite from a bank mortgage, which gives you money with no expectation other than you making your payments. If you make a million on the real estate transaction, the bank is not in your pocket with a percentage or a fee to close it out at maturity. A mortgage is a pure instrument where *you* use the *lender*. The advisory business uses outdated methods that use *you*.

Your Broker Is Usually Broker than You

Most financial advisors are order takers or salespeople. They know nothing about asset allocation, economics, behavioral finance, accounting or geopolitical risk. But they make your weighting decisions for you. They are not qualified to give tax advice, and yet they often do. If they had money of their own, they'd be trading for themselves full time. Of course, many advisors are fantastic people who do their job well—I can think of three or four I work with still who are very eager to help me, even though they are not subject-matter experts. Most advisors try to do right by their clients, but once the good ones figure out how things work, they quit and do it themselves. Why would you want to manage other people's money when you can build your own nest egg? Why would anyone want the headache of costing other people money as a zero-value-add?

I always ask my brokers difficult questions, even the best ones. I point out problems or contradictions in their plans so they have to go do research and get back to me. If they recommend something, I like to point out the bear case against it to play devil's advocate and to see if they're actually familiar with that particular opportunity. It's a gentle way to remind them that they don't have a clue what they're talking about. The irony is that the vast majority of financial advisors in the banking and asset management world are not qualified to give you financial advice. Good ones will be the first to admit this to you. Asking your broker about a stock is like asking your car salesman how to fix the transmission—you're simply speaking to the wrong person.

If this scenario resonates with you, educate yourself on the mechanics of starting a DIY couch-potato, low-fee index-fund portfolio. It's all about preserving your capital. An index-fund portfolio is cheaper, safer, and more efficient than a managed fund, and you won't have to listen to stock brokers eat their lunch on the phone ever again.

HOW THE RICH GET RICHER

The rich get richer. That's the nature of asset preservation. You could say it's up there with the law of gravity. As a rule, they're more educated, ambitious, and capable, but the fact is that they're also playing a completely different game than the average person. Independent traders from the masses have to walk into the bank to see Debbie the advisor for a 3 percent clip to underperform the biggest companies by half. The rich, on the other hand, can invest in hedge funds that pay out more than 30 percent a year. They buy equity and debt in private placements and debentures, they lend out private mortgages, and start charities and foundations to offset taxes owing. They take massive chances and hit the tenbaggers because they have access due to being in certain circles, events, or organizations. They're *in the room* and therefore *in the deal*.

Investing directly into businesses either through private equity financings or debentures is referred to as "private placements." Anyone can do this once accredited, and it's a critical piece of the puzzle to balance out your open stock market positions. You also get warrants that will often make the win a double win, with the option to buy another share for each one you bought in the private placement. This is usually referred to as a unit offering.

This allows you to liquidate your stock position mere months after buying and then "ride the warrants," which allows you to keep an "option" on the stock even though you have sold out of the position you bought. Basically, it came with a sweetener, which is another line in the water for that particular stock, even after you've sold your private placement stock.

You need to know, think, and act like a fund if you don't want one to rip your head off in your first year of trading. Getting a free warrant in a unit offering can be as good as a guaranteed double if you know what you're doing and you time it right. Warrants are typically also good for twelve to twenty-four months; they are an option, but not an obligation to buy the stock that can go in the filing cabinet for next year—remember that. When you take *you* out of the equation, that is often what makes the tenbagger happen.

Let your warrants grow and build equity over time. As you build up a treasure chest of warrants, you'll be amazed at how effective a model it can be, especially if you know how to play the short side of a stock. By buying your stock directly from the issuer, you avoid the "secondary market" (the stock market) altogether until you want to sell. This effectively turns you into private equity or a "merchant banker" to the issuing company because it's a role normally fulfilled by investment banks and family offices.

Congrats! You are now a bank.

It's an exclusive world, open to accredited investors only. The exact requirements for receiving accreditation and being able to do these things vary by region, but a rule of thumb is $250,000 or more of annual income and at least $1 million in personal net worth. That intentionally excludes 99 percent of the public, so accredited investors come from the remaining 1 percent. The irony is that once you're wealthy enough to become accredited, you become eligible to invest in investments that bear 20 to 30 percent a year, so you can become wealthier quicker than less well-off people, with less stress. Not only that, your fees are also much lower because people with money demand that their money is not pillaged and picked over like a regular civilian's is. It's like being offered the special bottle of scotch from under the bar without having to ask for the good stuff. You're an insider. You don't have to drink from the retail troughs ever again.

Becoming an accredited investor might be a process, but it is possible to do in a year, and it's sometimes possible to get around some of the requirements. Find a fee-based financial advisor and chartered accountant to help with it. Ask someone accredited who they go to for financial advice. Find someone who's a bit further ahead on their financial journey than you, and find out how they got there. Ask what tools have worked for them that you might be able to use. A simple referral to a good accountant can be an absolute game changer for a new investor, for example. If you don't have anyone to contact, and you have exhausted all options, contact me, and I will personally find somewhere you can go.

I have had many small private placements turn into tenbaggers. That's investing $25,000 directly into a company's private placement offering at a time when no one wants to support them (*high* risk) and then eventually selling the shares into the secondary market for $250,000 or more once the masses wake up to the opportunity.

That's how the rich get richer. They're there way before you are. They are usually FIFO: first in, first out. Retail investors are usually last in and last out.

Private capital opens up if you have a million bucks, and sometimes you can invest as little as $100,000 to play, but you have to be *accredited*. That's how you learn about the opportunities. Sometimes all you need is $100,000, which is a big sum of money, but not if you can get into a hedge fund managed by a proven entity. That's one of the easiest ways to find private investments before they're open to the public. My neighbor, who earns just under $250,000 per year, wouldn't be allowed in, as he's not accredited.

Accreditation amounts to a single-page waiver accepting that what you're buying is high risk and you could lose everything. But those are also the code words that will alert you to a potential ten-bagger if you can find the right ones at the right time. Could you lose everything? Of course! But go back to the books and reread about asset allocation so that if you *do* lose everything on that one bet, *it doesn't ruin you*. It simply provides you a tax loss for that year.

This is what the wealthy understand. Once you dial in your bite sizes and allocate properly, it's a relatively stress-free game since you can totally detach from the outcome and not depend on any one investment taking off. More importantly, there is no one trade or investment going to zero that could badly harm your overall position. And you take the losses where you get them once you are properly balanced and allocated, as they help with your tax bill at the end of the year.

When I look back and analyze where I best performed, it was when I focused on making quality long-term bets on proven operators by way of private placements. I went to networking events, I met good leaders and CEOs, and they offered me stock in their own company. I invested a good amount with a long-term angel-investor-type approach, and I came out much further ahead than if I had simply bought a chunk of their common stock on the open market. There are three reasons for this success. First, there was a period when I was forced to hold so that the stock could go up more without me having the option to sell any. Second, I was able to buy at a discount to the market, as the private placement price is usually lower than the market price. And lastly, I was given a full warrant, effectively giving me a two-for-one if the stock continued to perform to the upside.

These opportunities don't come easy, and they don't come often, but they are out there happening every day: you just have to find yourself in a room and then in a deal. Always be advised that while it is wise to scale quietly in and out of the open market, it is much more important in a situation where you invest directly into the company in a private placement. You cannot be seen as clunky, or you will never be invited in again. Every company wants a healthy and functioning market, so ensure that, if and when you step out, you do so like a gentleman and exit as the liquidity permits. This means no bid hitting and using tools at your disposal like anonymous and iceberg orders if appropriate.

The company will not like seeing Anonymous selling a little bit of stock every day, but remember that the company works for *you*, the shareholder, not the other way around. Be transparent and tell them it's you selling and that you will only sell X amount per day. If they can't respect you as a small seller, then their respect for you as a potential buyer was conditional, and your money doesn't need that drama. Scale out and move on to the next venture, and find one that isn't obsessed with who might be selling their stock on any given day. Hold the warrants in case that company gets bought out in the future and move on.

The system is built against the masses to protect and insulate the wealthy. Many people inside the system will admit it's built to shift economics from the poor toward the wealthy, especially during downturns, which are often referred to as periods of "wealth transfer." That's a great eye-opener for a lot of people, but an independent trader needs to know that the machine is rigged for the house. As long as you act like a retailer rather than an institution, you are willingly getting fee'd to death while supporting the giant money machine.

It's time to start calling fees what they really are: fines. Fines for the naive and for the poor. If you have a load of cash in your account, your fees are minimal. I don't pay fees unless I have to. Most of the time, if you ask for them to be waived, they are. If you aren't getting any luck there, then move to an institution that will acknowledge your value to them.

Beware of the Banks

It might seem that I'm being hard on the banks—but the banking system has a sinister side. For some context about the origins of the Western banking system and its owners, read the jaw-dropping 1994 book about the Federal Reserve "cartel" called *The Creature From Jekyll Island* by G. Edward Griffin. *It could be the most important book about money you ever read.* If you're a serious investor, you'll want to know what caused the creation of the Federal Reserve in 1913 in the first place and who created it. What did it have to do with World War I, which began right after? And what role did the banks play in World War II.

Remember that You're Already Rich

As we've already seen, the fundamental difference between a poor man and a rich man is simply that the poor man spends more than he earns. That's it; that's all there is to it.

My grandfather never made more than $60,000 a year in the military, and he retired very comfortably at sixty-five, with two homes fully paid for, a small airplane, a great lifestyle, and regular vacations. He was never a high earner, but he retired a wealthy man.

His son, my father, earned around $250,000 per year as an airport tower manager and air traffic controller, and he never had a dollar to speak of. No vacations, no new cars, nothing, let alone any investments or real assets. He could not make ends meet, and he spent every check before it got to his bank account on the latest tech gadgets, expensive tools he never used, booze, ciggies, and lottery tickets. He died at fifty-two years old with literally nothing. He was a high earner, and yet he lived the life of a poor man.

This gave me an interesting look into our relationship with the money people generate.

My father's relationship with money was completely out of whack. Despite his large income and no significant bills, he had a serious poverty mindset. Money was elusive to him. It was "for the rich," even though he generated a million dollars every four years. He was intimidated by money; he didn't feel worthy of it for some reason, so it fell through his fingers like a handful of water.

Grampa was a lifelong aviator, and he knew that fiat currency was nothing more than fuel. Go-juice for life stuff. He didn't love it or hate it; he just used it effectively and efficiently so that it did not use him. To him, money was a sort of indicator of doing the right thing: work hard, work well, be honest, treat others well...and expect an abundant life. The money is only good if you trade it for the things that matter for you and those around you. If you exchange it for beer and ciggies every day, then it might get tired of being used improperly and move on to someone who is more attentive toward its energy.

People have been saying for more than two thousand years that fools and their money are soon parted, but it's still true—now more than ever—and unless you understand that, you'll always wind up chasing it and feeling like you don't *have* it. You need to focus on properly protecting what you have, first and foremost. Ancient Chinese rice traders had rules to insulate their wealth. They properly protected their *own* rice in the warehouse rather than worrying about how to get some of their neighbor's rice.

Remember that you're already rich. Now it's your job to build *wealth*. You can't do that if you're always being aggressive or loose with the money you've earned. If you treat it like a drunk, it's going to treat you the same way.

Focus on capital preservation by not giving your money to a banking system that has little interest in looking after it. Educate yourself today. Focus on two or three areas that you need improvement on and buy a few books or hop on YouTube to watch a few hours of educational videos. You could download a free Excel spreadsheet template of an asset allocation tool and start to map out on paper your next check or source of income, and where it's going to go. Start to monitor the cash flow in and out, and notice what sticks out for you. Are you paying yourself first? Or does zero percent on average go toward saving or investing or education? Does 100 percent of your income get "spent" within ten to fifteen days of you getting it? Let's start there: until you get your arms around this first, the other components will be elusive.

Know When to Cut a Loss

"Be fearful when others are greedy and
greedy when others are fearful."

—WARREN BUFFETT

When Warren Buffett made his famous observation about investing, he meant not to let FOMO drag you into doing what everyone else is doing, just because everyone else is doing it. Years of data about mutual funds show that the public has a remarkable ability to buy in most aggressively at the very top of market cycles, then get out and panic-sell as soon as the market crashes and bottoms out. It's in our nature. It's human behavior to fight, flight, or freeze to survive. People have an uncanny ability to buy at the top and sell at the bottom.

By simply knowing and reminding yourself of this, you can avoid many disastrous outcomes before they even begin.

The market works in cycles. In early September 2021, the market was near a peak, and the public was bullish. That's when the smart money quietly started going to cash and more "risk-off" bets. When the general public is screaming from the rooftops about Dogecoin and GameStop, you know the market is starting to get top-heavy after the tremendous move up in prices over the past twenty years.

It's only going to go one way. Since as far back as 1928, the year before the Wall Street crash, the end of every market cycle has been marked by the same warning indicators: insiders and institutions selling, wealthy people hedging and de-risking, and the masses piggishly piling into the markets for the very first time.

Follow the smart money. Ignore the blind masses.

Personally, I'm too much of a contrarian to follow the herd; it's not in my nature. If you say go, I stop. That's what rebels without causes do: they resist. They're stoners, they're bikers, they're pilots, they're rogue stock traders and activist investors. They stubbornly go against the public perception in the pursuit of individual freedoms, feelings, and convictions.

Let Your Winners Run, and Cut Your Losses Early

"The coward dies a thousand deaths,
the brave but one."

—ERNEST HEMINGWAY

Accept defeat, move on. Do not die on this hill, but live to fight another day.

Holding losers is gut-wrenching every day you look at your account. If you see a loser that was never supposed to go red on you, cut it quick before it's too late and you lose more. And if you think something's gonna run, get out of the way. Again, be mindful of time frames. If this is "forever," then why are you even looking at it? And if it's a good trade gone bad, then why are you still holding it?

It's Kenny Rogers gambling. You have to know when to hold them and know when to fold them.

It's so hard to walk away. It's human nature. As soon as I've doubled my money at a table game, I put my initial stake back in my pocket. That way I'm only playing with house money. If I win, I win. If I lose, I still didn't lose a dime of my original bet. It was free entertainment (or stress) after that point.

If all blackjack players did that, there would be no casinos.

You can do the exact same thing with stocks. Make a double? Sell half! Ride the rest for free.

It's the same battle with crypto and with shares. "I'll give it another day" or "I'll see how it does next week." It's hard to walk away because a time will come when you *are* ahead. Anyone can make a modest gain and give it back. The trick is knowing when to stop. That's how professional poker players bully amateurs by slowly bleeding them out. It's like starting with $100,000 and setting out to make 10 percent: it's relatively easy. It's all about asset allocation, money management, and knowing the risks.

"I'll just wait until my luck turns around." Forget luck. You need a strategy—a plan.

LIVE IN THE GRAY

At one stage of the initial cannabis boom, I thought security and banking solutions were lacking in the industry, so I took a liking to a small startup firm in Ontario called 3 Sixty Secure. I bought into their story and kept buying at seventy-five cents per share as the news releases kept pointing to all the good news. When the price began to fall, I doubled down, much like the solar venture a few years earlier. When it tanked to 10 cents, I listened to the CEO's sociopathic sales pitches and bought again and again as the price fell even more. Suddenly, I was the biggest buyer of the stock... and then the only buyer, which I held across five different accounts— never use one account to try and save another one, ever—until one day, all trading in 3 Sixty Secure was halted due to insufficient financial reporting. Eventually, it was suspended and then delisted as it went to zero. Thanks for coming out.

It remains that way to this day—dead. Every time I check my accounts, I still see the losses frozen at a deep six figures for a stock that I couldn't even sell at a penny if I wanted to. It's a continual mocking reminder of a time when I should have walked away but was instead lazily looking for a quick gain. Everyone in the Toronto banking scene was telling me what a hero I'd be when the market came back and I listened. It'll never come back. And those iBankers have long moved on to create more smash-and-grab startup schemes just like 3 Sixty. I was their liquidity. I was the only player big enough and stupid enough to buy their story.

Coulda, woulda, shoulda... That's why you never throw big Hail Marys unless you are damn sure that the risk of losing everything is minimal.

Three Sixty Secure was one of my biggest losses, up there with 1933 Industries. It was a perfect example of why you shouldn't try to be a hero. I was selling off my good stuff so I could buy more of it every time the price fell further. I was waiting for a market that never came, while the unapologetic and conniving CEO was accused by his own board of buying personal items with the corporate treasury. Every time I texted him, he just poured out the great news, told me I would be wise to be buying stock, and sprinkled some FOMO. He never once mentioned any of the trials and tribulations that were going on. Whenever I log into my brokerage account, that frozen account is a reminder that I should have asked much harder questions. When you speak to CEOs, make sure they tell you what they are most worried about. That's the only way you can decide for yourself if their stressors are enough to stay away from the company as an investment.

I already had enough 3 Sixty Secure stock one month into the multiyear saga. I should have given it a year to see what happened. I didn't need to buy it every day and seek out validation. That was just my compulsion. I was addicted to buying 3 Sixty stock the same way I was addicted to trying to turn around 1933 Industries by buying its stock every chance I got.

I treated both like they were black-and-white situations. I should have been living in the gray. My entire life has been a lesson that there is no black and white, only shades of grey. Life is far from binary, and trading is not about buying and selling. It's about living in the gray, wading in and wading out of the water, so you are never really in or out. It's about being in *accumulation mode* or *distribution mode* or somewhere in between.

The second you say, "Fuck it, I'm in," you're making a mistake. And the second you say, "Fuck it, I'm out," you're making another mistake. The very second you make a move that requires you to admit that you're probably wrong means you're dead wrong and that you're going to lose. Try wading in and wading out. There are no right and wrong decisions, only a series of choices.

Compulsive stock investors are black-and-white thinkers, just like compulsive gamblers. The best investors know that investing is not binary at all. It's like any other form of gambling or speculating: you don't put your whole bankroll on the table, particularly if you're being talked into it or, worse, doing it due to any sort of coercion or peer pressure.

Imagine playing dice in elementary school, and the school-yard bully talks you into putting the entirety of your lunch money down for a roll. That's the same as letting a stock-market pirate or executive talk you into buying shares of their company with the very money that feeds your family. Or worse yet, giving their stock promotion the only dollars you have.

Trust Your Intuition More

If you make a reputation as an investor, people start coming to you with opportunities, so be careful. They want your money, and they want your name on the shareholder list. They want to use your name to sell more shares to others who may know you. I get bombarded with pitch decks for the latest and greatest solution every day. I ignore most of them, but it's difficult if it involves someone with whom I have some sort of a friendship or any other connection. As a people pleaser, it's all too easy to get sucked into considering their "exciting opportunity" because you don't want to be rude. Never allow this to happen to you. Take the meeting because *you* want to, not because *they* want you to. Your time is too precious, and it does not belong to them.

I say no to meetings I don't want to take that could easily waste four hours of my time. That initial meeting can turn into a series of emails, secondary meetings, and then hours of trying to get them to go away when you could have said no from the outset. Tune your intuition to protect your time.

Make Good Choices and Avoid Bad People

It's taken me a lifetime to learn to ignore a text message from someone who I know is a time waster. A lot of training in self-respect and boundaries. For a bullied kid, being put on a pedestal is hard to ignore. They need money, I have some money, and they say things I can't say no to. Boundaries are probably the most important thing for survival and success in investing.

It's important to say no often—and to mean it. Otherwise, you'll learn to live with dis-ease because the stress will make you physically ill. The mind-body connection is incredibly real and incredibly strong. The documentary *E-Motion* tells the story of Joe Dispenza, who was left paraplegic by a cycling accident. Joe was told he was never going to walk again, but he refused to accept it. Now he lectures around the world about freeing yourself from your mind. Steve Jobs was told he had six months to live with a rare form of pancreatic cancer. He went on an alkaline diet and lived another eight years. Wayne Dyer developed leukemia but learned to live with it and lived many more years than his team of medical professionals said was possible.

The connection of mind, body, and your investing is important in terms of protecting your beginnings—your time and your finances.

HALF CORRECT IS STILL WRONG

You need to learn to say no. It's the most powerful word in our language. I realized that the only people that really matter are my wife and my kids. So now I only make decisions that will benefit them. Period. My time in Vegas robbed me of countless events with my kids, but the trade for me is that now, if the opportunity came along again, it would take me a fraction of a second to say, "No. I'm going to pass on that one."

Protect your beginnings.

If something is causing you grief, decide whether or not you actually need it in your life right now. Why would I jeopardize the life I built for this undue stress that someone or something has put on me? Remember that even if you say no *now*, you can ultimately say *yes* later. So do yourself a favor and practice some strict nos in your investing and trading, especially if market participants are trying to coerce you into buying their story or stock. If you say no now, chances are you'll be able to buy into it later anyways, and likely cheaper. Imagine what that type of patience could do for your portfolio and for your peace of mind.

When I look back at the guys who were getting me to buy into their companies, they were always trying to build something for themselves that I had already built for myself. But I still jumped in their puddles out of people pleasing, curiosity, a genuine desire to help, and FOMO. These are toxic ingredients for investment. Don't build other people's wealth at the detriment of your own.

You Have to Be Able to Accept Defeat

Accept that selling off a losing position can and will make you *feel* like a loser, but also that you're not a loser. You cannot win every hand at the table. It's impossible. The mindset of a lot of people is never to admit to making a mistake—this is deadly. In the market, that attitude will wipe out your trading account.

Practice acceptance. Admit that you lost. It's a kind of spiritual, Buddhist approach, but it is practical too. The Tao teaches you to let things be, because once you accept what is, you can move on. You can do what needs to be done. If you don't accept it, it will fester and rot. So you sold the stock and moved on, but you didn't accept it. Now it's hanging over every single trade you do and polluting your process.

Without acceptance, I'd be at the bottom of a bottle right now. I have a lot of friends who, when I share even just a shred of my losses, ask me, "How do you handle losing money like that?" I tell them it's the cost of admission. It's part of the process. It's the cost of tuition for my investor's PhD. It's not cheap because it's proven to be effective.

As long as you trade, you have to be willing to accept a certain amount of loss. Sometimes it's bigger, sometimes it's smaller, but if you can't accept that, close this book and please do not get into this game—for your sake and that of your family. If you lose at the horse races or in the casino, and it throws you for a loop, don't get into the markets. You're going to end up paying with your personal health and well-being, and *nothing* on earth is worth that. An investor or speculator unable to accept defeat when he needs to is a ticking time bomb. You need to learn acceptance at the level of a great warrior—one who can cut through whatever story he may have about the error and move forward on his broader mission. Like animals that are done fighting, you need to forget and move on if you want to be prepared for and survive the next battle.

There's nothing to be gained by going back over old wounds except for some journal time to physically write down what went wrong so that you may spot it in advance next time.

The answer to all of life's problems is acceptance.

And no problem is a real problem if it can be solved with money.

Take Profit When the
Trade Is Good

Sometimes it's difficult to recognize success in investing.

The trick is recognizing when a trade is good. Ask yourself, "If I'm up 30 percent in a year on a trade that I was only looking for 15 percent return on in six months, did I do good? Or is there more to come? Am I being foolish for holding on this late?" If you bought the stock with the intention of never selling and you're up 30 percent, why on earth would you consider selling it now? If you lock in the 30 percent and in another twelve months it's up 60 percent from your cost basis, you'll feel like you made a huge mistake. On the flip side, if you had a six-month timeline on the trade and on month thirteen it goes back to a 15 percent gain, then you wasted six months watching the overbaked trade that was good on month six. Sticking to your timeline is *everything*.

It's not a simple equation you can work out either. A profit on paper does not necessarily mean you should sell. *Trading is not binary.* If you think it is, I promise that you are doing it wrong and that you will soon find out why. There are dichotomies everywhere when trading and investing; this is where art meets science. You need a plan so that you know when your trade is good, so that you *know what a win looks like.* Knowing how and when to exit a trade is as important as knowing how to enter it.

A BIRD IN THE HAND

If you make a stellar trade execution, you might think, "I'm going to buy more and do that again." But sometimes it's better to book that win and start the cooldown before you fire the jets back up. Call it a clear head, or that little sorbet you get between courses of a meal to clear the palate. Just as you have to cut and run from a bad trade, you also need to debrief yourself from a good trade. Find out where you went right. On the golf course, whether you finish the hole with a triple-bogey or a birdie, you still need to walk to the next tee box and hit a good drive again, despite any negative emotions or adrenaline. Find your sorbet after a good trade and tune into the energy and decisions that got you there. Now you know that you can do it, so study it and learn to replicate your successful trades. After a while, they'll start to look very mundane and very similar; that's called being a professional.

Buy stocks over time and sell them over time so that you operate in accumulation mode or distribution mode buying and selling in tranches, never the whole position at once. This key ingredient is always what is lacking in amateurs who are wondering why they can't seem to stop losing money trading. It's their timing, yes, but it's more determined by their weighting. When a fund or activist wants to make a move into Boeing or General Motors, they simply cannot, nor would they ever, buy their stock in one trade ticket. They tell their brokers to start accumulating quietly so as to not disrupt the market or show their cards.

If you go in heavy handed, you're going to move the stock and pay more than you had to. Trading is messy as all hell when it gets clunky. It's a game of finesse that requires a certain sure-footedness, and it seemingly always rejects the heavy-footed operators. You have to dance with the market on its own terms just as you would with the wind and the waves in a sailboat.

Don't See Your Position as a Snapshot; See It as a Trend

If a stock is weak and your bias is to sell, figure out how you'll start to distribute back to the market over a period of time. Do not try and time the market; instead, use time to your advantage. If you step out too quickly, you could spook the market, the price would then fall, and you'll suffer financial cannibalism as a result.

Take advantage of time. That's something the world's greatest investors all say repeatedly. Nothing is as important for investors and speculators as time. *Use time* instead of letting it use you. Sit on the bid for something you really like for a year or more. I bought many of my best trades over the course of a year. It's statistically proven that you can make significantly more gains if you have the discipline not to touch the offer but rather sit and wait on the bid while also saving a relatively significant percentage of money on the bid-ask spread.

Behavior with the bid-ask is another bit of wisdom that separates the smart money—expert traders, banks, and institutions— from the dumb money, which is everyone else who is not familiar with this valuable data point.

Dumb money is people sitting with their iPad staring out the window trying to process what to do. You're the dumb money if you find yourself in that position. You're at the end of the retail chain, standing in the line at Walmart. But you can change that for good if you start trading like an institution does. You can change it overnight.

Create a Roadmap and Define What It Means to Be Successful

Don't try to be a hero. Keep your head down so it doesn't get shot off. And don't let your ADD interfere with your trading, because if you enjoy trading financial instruments, chances are you likely have some sort of attention deficit disorder and probably don't even realize it. That's why you buy Ethereum or Shiba Inu coin on Monday, and on Wednesday, you want out. Thursday you get back in as it goes back up, then you sell it on Friday when the market tanks two points, only to see it higher again the following Monday. Your flawed squirrel brain is changing the plan and getting in the way of sound business practice. Worse yet, these bad habits can and will go on for months and years if you don't step in and save your portfolio from neurotic trading habits.

Stick to the script and don't change course too easily. A ship doesn't change its destination port on the fly because the captain decides one morning to go somewhere else. That causes chaos and costs money for everyone else involved.

So if you buy ABC stock and it goes up 20 percent, did you win? Or are you only halfway to your 40 percent target? Only *you* know, and only *you* can decide. Define what a profitable trade looks like *before* you buy the stock. Be like an athlete. Make sure you can visualize success and that you know what it looks like; otherwise, you lose before you start.

In fact, it's impossible to be successful in business if you can't visualize and recognize success. Professional athletes visualize better than anyone else because champions know it's an absolute requirement to make victory happen. You can't win the cup if you don't see it and pull those thoughts into your own reality. Tiger Woods once said, "If I can't see the ball going into the hole before the shot, how can I expect it to go in?" It's all visualization. When the basketball left Michael Jordan's fingertips, he envisioned the basket every single time. When Wayne Gretzky took the shot, he always visualized the puck going into the net. These three greats expected success *every time*, and often got it as a result. It is not a coincidence that all sports greats say the same thing about expecting the outcome; they also say that the moment doubt creeps in, no matter how small, the shot is lost before it is taken.

It's called *The Power of Intention*, which is also a monumental 2004 book by Wayne Dyer.

Trading stocks is much the same. Many professional stock jockeys use the same visualization technique with their stock movements.

How to Parlay

The Supreme Cannabis Company was my first investment on the deal side of things. I'd never invested $40,000 directly into a company until Supreme. When it turned into $80,000 and then $90,000, I took it out. I sold like the rookie that I was, as soon as I saw the 100 percent win. I swiftly parlayed that money into Aurora, which generously became $300,000, which I put into CannaRoyalty, which then turned into $1 million in less than two years after I cut the original check into Supreme. I put that million from Canna-Royalty, now called Origin House, into 1933 Industries.

That turned it back into $300,000 a year later.

I parlayed perfectly from Supreme and then perfectly again, then a third time, and then I got piggish. I didn't take a coffee break, and made a rushed and sloppy fourth move that took me back two steps.

The secret recipe of funds, pensions, and high-net-worth investors is parlaying effectively—knowing how to move your chips about in a wavelike manner, knowing how to scale out when the storm is coming. If you make a profit, it might be time to move on to the next opportunity or hide out in cash for a while.

When you parlay, you're gambling with house money, not your own money. That first private placement investment of $40,000 in 2013 turned into upward of $7 or $8 million inside ten years due to a total of about 200 small, properly allocated private placements and more than 20,000 individual stock trades. And only the first $40,000 was mine. The rest came from Mr. Market due to repeated sound financial decisions.

The $40,000 I had given to the leverage-hungry advisor back when I started out is still worth –$60,000. The difference is that, back then, I was trying to get money for nothing. I also put all the money I had into one bet, all at once. So I was breaking two of my own rules.

Once you start parlaying effectively, you can turn next to nothing into something, as long as you have your asset allocation dialed in. Each time you make a good bet, you parlay your winnings. People use excuses like, "I don't have money," "I don't have an education," or "I don't have a wealthy family." You don't need any of those. I had none of those things. You just need a few opportunities and the ability to see them when they come to you. I started with $1,000 from my shitty jobs as a youngster, and I lost it down to zero at least a hundred times over before I even got the $40,000 to get into Supreme. The first few stages, going from

$4,000 to $40,000, were the holy grail: a tenbagger. An increase of 1,000 percent. After that, I knew I could play bigger and that the hardest part was now behind me. I had some working capital, which, if allocated properly and managed effectively, could turn into $400,000—at which point I would have some runway and have new options open up to me.

It took eighteen months of discipline and many pages of journaling to get there, but I did it, and I did it solo. You only need one of those trades to feel like you have a real foundation. When I had $40,000, I thought, "Wow, I'm an investor. No matter how small, at least I am in the game." That was all the runway I needed to allow me to become a full-time investor a short period later.

It all goes back to the bird in the hand. How do you know when you should lock in or realize profits as opposed to letting them ride? You don't, and you never will! So you determine if the story back when you bought it is still intact, measure that against your current plan, and check your weighting and timing. Does everything indicate hold, meaning that you'll simply want to own this asset tomorrow if you sell it today? Or does the analysis indicate that you can never go broke by taking a profit now and repeating this winning recipe on the next trade?

Either way, it's not black and white, so scale in or out accordingly.

One good, well-executed trade per year can give you an amazing life. Several bad trades in a year should make you reevaluate your entire strategy.

IT'S A PROCESS, NOT AN ACTION

Parlaying, asset allocation, money management, a plan, and conviction. Put them all in place, with discipline, and trading works beautifully. Yes, it can be hard to keep that discipline, but your trading plan is like a diet. You don't make random decisions day by day. You buy into the program and you stick to it without cheating; otherwise, you'll spin in circles.

Keep your eyes on the macro picture if you love a particular company or sector right now. The micro view is the details about the company from the ground up. The macro is the view from thirty thousand feet, top-down. It's why you wanted to own the stock in the first place. It's what you write in your trading journal to explain to yourself why you want to own this right now *and* in the future. From there, you can start your micro research. Speak to the CEO, ask hard questions, and get to know the balance sheet. Know their social media accounts and be familiar with their website, investor outreach, and messaging. Walk into their store and buy the products. How would you feel being an ambassador for them? This is how you start to get a sense of whether the stock is cheap or expensive based on all the available data and the competitive landscape. Is it oversold (when it's trading beneath what you think is its true value) or the opposite, overbought? Are people eager to buy it or are they indifferent?

Remember: trading is a zero-sum game. The price depends on whether there are more sellers or buyers on any particular day. The stock is slowly being pushed higher or lower, so you need to know where you are on the chart in terms of recent price action. Follow the daily volume for at least a month before you get involved emotionally or financially.

These are your tools: the broader trends, human behavior, macro trends, microeconomics, the competitive landscape, boots-on-the-ground due diligence, the technical indicators, and the fundamentals, which are the hard facts: the balance sheet, the assets, the income statement, the sales, the revenue, the margins. Like a doctor, you need the whole picture to be able to diagnose properly.

When I started buying Experion in early 2020, I'd watched it trade for *more than two years* without doing a thing. I watched go from $1.75 in late 2017 to $0.75 in late 2018, to $0.10 in late 2019. In January 2020, I started buying at $0.07 knowing full well that nothing had actually changed, except for a 180-degree shift in investor sentiment, taking it from almost $2.00 to almost worthless while the management team had no tools to stop the selling or knowledge to get people excited enough to buy.

I knew the target inside and out, and I knew that, unless it went under, it would go back to $0.25 or greater once sentiment shifted and the pendulum swung the other way. I knew that the same fear driving people to hit the bid today would be back full circle in the form of greed shortly, when they would be buying stock off the offer.

So I got in my car and I drove to the back hills of Mission, British Columbia, to see the CEO. I said, "Tell me the good, the bad, and the ugly. I want to know what keeps you up at night. And I want to know what you're excited about."

Short answer: the industry was down, but the business was

actually up. Micro good, macro less so. The CEO told me, "Our sales are up, and we are attracting the right talent. We have capital. We have zero debt on the balance sheet. We're opening up new sales channels every quarter."

The sector was optically and energetically shit, but the company was in tremendous shape. I figured that the worst-case scenario was that the industry was going to continue to be challenging, but that Experion would outperform it and appear rosy on the back end. My gut was that the micro was more important than the macro in this case, considering my horizon was over a year.

That time, I was right—but only because I checked every single due-diligence box and put in all the required work, like a surgeon does before an incision is made.

Don't Sell Your Winners to Buy Your Losers

When they see a stock turn red or green, most people's plan changes. That's human nature. They go back to the drawing board, and they usually fall flat on their face. They allow fear and greed to come in as soon as their position moves, and they get emotional. The stock goes green, and they think, "Great, three thousand bucks. Chop it." But they meant to own it for a whole year, so now they have to waste energy and commissions and fees getting back in, often at higher prices, defeating the whole purpose of selling in the first place.

Always, always, always know the answer to "Why do I own this?" It's an effective little test to see if you should be in the trade or not, especially when it comes to cryptocurrencies and microcap stocks.

Each time you buy, you can also plan to be down right off the bat by about 1 percent of the position, due to brokerage fees and the bid-ask spread.

A stock goes red, and people think, "I can buy more, and I can help get it back up." Or "I can buy more because it's cheaper." That's dollar-cost averaging, and it should be reserved for important, long-term investments, which does not apply to a rental stock, option, or crypto trade that has gone against you.

Know the trends and understand whether something is trending cheaper or more expensive and why. That will allow your mind and your spirit to balance your natural instincts. You have to understand whether you're buying cheap or at a premium. It's like clothing. You can overpay for Gucci because you want to own the name, or you can go to a no-name store and buy value without any name recognition or popularity.

There are value investors, who like to buy for pennies on the dollar, and there are growth investors, who are willing to overpay for things that are going to continue to move higher. Ask yourself where you fit. What gives you harmony? What excites you in your day-to-day life: a great deal or a popular product?

Never Trade on Tips, News, or Hype

It's the big race at the biggest meeting of the year. You're standing in line at the window, waiting to place your bet. You've studied the form for weeks. You tracked the horses, trainers, and jockeys and kept charts of how they're doing. You know which owners are on a streak. You studied yesterday's results for final confirmation of today's action.

You've picked your horse. Golden Nugget, each way. Depending on your resources, you might bet $1,000, even $10,000.

The horse's odds are shortening as the race gets closer, but you ignore them. You've done your due diligence, and changing odds don't alter any of the data you've studied for weeks to make your choice today.

Golden Nugget, all the way.

Then, when you're one or two people away from the window, you hear a guy behind you say, "Did you see them in the parade ring? That Long Shot looks like a hell of a horse!"

So you ask the guy, "How did Golden Nugget look?"

"Skittish. Hot. Not looking great today."

Fuck.

And when you finally reach the window, you hand over your money, and on an impulse you say, "Long Shot, to win." Months of prep were just steamrolled and ignored for a five-second speculative, emotionally driven, and subjective conversation with some rookie you don't even know, who might have 1/100th of the time you spent committed to this race.

We all know the rest of the story. Long Shot falls apart out there, Golden Nugget wins by a length, and you never see your money again. You should have won, and you would have won, but you let your own emotion demolish all your hard work one minute before decision time.

It's human nature. We hear something we believe is inside knowledge, a tip no one else knows, and all our hard work goes out the window. We don't even know the guy in the line, but we can't help wondering if he knows better than us. We're all so desperate to be on the inside, to learn the short cut to the quick high, that anyone is ready in an instant to go, "Fuck my plan, I'm just going to do this."

Call It What It Really Is: Losing

Call it impulse. Call it FOMO. Call it suggestibility or peer pressure. There are lots of deep psychological reasons why it's so difficult to resist tips from someone else—a stock commentary on TV, a barber, a friend, someone in the bar or at the beach, even a total stranger standing in line. Something deep within our psyche makes us want to act on information we somehow feel is privileged.

But call it what it really is: *losing*. You change your bet at the last second, and you lose everything. It's a loser move, and it's statistically not going to work out well for you.

Never trade on tips, news, or hype. I simply cannot stress this enough.

No one who bets seriously on sports would rely on that kind of off-the-cuff, hair-trigger decision. No professional gambler could survive like that. You wouldn't put your money in a bank if you thought the advisor might invest it on the basis of something he overheard in the elevator that morning.

Why be any different when you trade yourself?

KNOW THE FACTS

With trading, gathering information is just half the story; the other half is acting upon it. That's your responsibility—to yourself, to your family, to the business.

In the market, the only hard facts are the numbers on the screen, blinking and changing green or red, but the ether is full of noise: rumors and whispers, nods and winks, tips and insights. It's full of leaks, hints, and apparently well-meaning folks who are seemingly desperate to help you succeed—or perhaps to convince you of the very same thing they're trying to convince themselves of. When they're not sure, they're miserable, and everyone knows that misery loves company.

And that well-meaning guy at the track who gave you a tip? At least he *thought* he was helping. In the market, for every person who means well, there are a dozen more who positively mean you harm. That's no exaggeration. They need your trades for them to make their money, and they profit as your trades get filled. For them, you're just another bid that's going to pay for their kids to go to private school.

They're shysters in suits. There's a good chance that the better cut the suit, the bigger the shyster.

If You Can't Identify the Stupidest Person in the Room, It's You

How can you tell the shysters from the good guys? The only sure-fire way is to cut out the noise and listen only within, after you've done your work. The shysters are the sirens who'll draw you onto the rocks. They don't have your interests at heart, just their own. They're like the merchants in California in 1849 who realized that digging for gold was a mug's game when there was an even bigger fortune to be made by selling picks and shovels to the idiots who didn't realize that *they* were the mugs.

It's like any other part of life. If you don't know who the mug is, it's probably you.

Too many independent traders get disoriented by the noise. They see tickers on the TV screen, they get anonymous tips direct from their Twitter feed, they hear Jim Cramer pushing this or that company (the same guy who told everyone to keep their money in Bear Stearns in March of 2008, months before it went bankrupt in September), and they buy into this crap because they think it's a short cut. The easier way or maybe the path of least resistance.

Yeah, it's a short cut. Like flipping a coin or a Ponzi scheme. What the folks in the market know but you don't realize is that once you're trading on tips, news, or hype, you've *become* the volume. You've become a liquidity maker, and you don't even know it. Your money is nothing but fuel to keep the market moving. As soon as you put your money in, it's gone. It's become one of a million little stepping stones for other people to drive up the value of their assets.

The problem is that this insider stuff appeals to the emotions, and emotion is never your friend when you're sitting in front of a trading screen.

THE END OF THE BUBBLE

When your barber or kids' little league coach starts giving you stock tips, you're tempted to listen and hear them out because you're surprised to hear regular civilians talk stock. For a stock investor, it's very hard not to want to engage in that kind of conversation. But their eagerness should get your defenses up. Whenever the bottom of the financial food chain starts looking to bet on stocks, that means the market has fallen into bubble territory. People get emotionally attached to the idea of hitting it big on some stock or crypto buy because everyone else is seemingly "getting into the market." They're frightened to miss out on "easy money," if there is such a thing. Remember the joke in the stock business that's been true since the 1920s: when the guy in the elevator or the doorman gives you stock tips, you're at the end of the money line. It happened in 1929, in 1987, in 1999, and in 2008. The public got into the market the last year of the cycle, right before the bust.

In 1999, everyone was rushing to sell their homes to put money into newly listed dot-com startups on the NASDAQ. They didn't even check the business plan of these companies; otherwise, they would have found out that those "businesses" didn't have a plan. The guys that made money in those times were not trading on tips or hype; instead, they were betting on a sure thing. They have a system they've created over the years. When the poorest people who got in last jump back out at the bottom of the market, those pros in there are shaking the tree, picking up the cheap shares that the amateurs just paid a huge premium for a short while before.

They confirmed again exactly what mutual funds have demonstrated for almost a century: that the public has an incredible ability to buy the top and sell out once the market bottoms out. That leaves the pros and institutions the luxury of liquidity at the

MONEY MIND

top and lots of cheap inventory to buy at the bottom.

I watched the meme stock pandemonium through 2021 and was reminded that these manias never end well. They ruin lives. I tried it myself over fifteen years ago when I set up StockSyndicate.com. I wanted to recruit a million little guys like me so we could become an army of activist investors. But the GameStop swarm had no leader and thus no tip to its spear. They had no education. They didn't even have any money. Just like with Bitcoin, people got involved to feel a sense of pride. They don't want to read the manuals; they just want to know what to buy and when. They are blind, sniffing around for a free truffle in the dark.

I recognized my own eighteen-year-old brain in those twenty-something GME-to-the-moon kids. And I felt sorry for them because they all craved diamond hands (conviction) and wanted easy gains—instant gratification in the laziest way. It's the very opposite of what I call investment. It's being blind and piggish, waving your last twenty bucks at the horse race with a beer in one hand and an empty wallet in the back of your jeans. They don't even realize that when they're playing on the market, they're up against infinitely more advanced bots, algorithms, and hedge funds. They're going into battle without a weapon or any training. They are going to get slaughtered when the enemy decides to strike.

Things will have to change when nineteen-year-olds are able to buy short-term options contracts on their phone using leverage with buying power coming from their credit card—with zero market experience or net worth. That only happens when you enter everything-bubble territory: the end of the tracks where every asset class has gotten expensive because there is too much cheap credit and way too much excess buying power floating around.

This Is Exactly Why I'm Writing This Book

When I started trading, I had to go through pages and pages of KYC (know your client) paperwork, printed out and signed in ink, to open a brokerage account. Now it takes five minutes on a phone. That will have to change because trading is too serious to be treated that loosely. No one would enter into a real estate contract on their cell phone just because they feel like it after reading a Reddit post. But that's precisely what people do with equities. It's dangerous that something as serious as buying into the share capital of a large business listed on Wall Street has been gamified. I'm all for trends that give more power to the little guy, but it should be done seriously, not in a yolo-a-meme-stock cynical manner.

Trading an online account doesn't feel as real as money in your hand: it's easy to get desensitized. It's the difference between putting $500 for dinner on a credit card, which is easy, versus counting out $500 in bills from your wallet. Taking out the bills *feels* more expensive because there is sensory input from your hands to your mind. It's the exact opposite of desensitization. Imagine what would happen to retail shopping centers or the restaurant industry if there were no credit or debit cards? I'll let you look up what percent of transactions are done on the Visa, Mastercard, or Amex network.

In 2005, when I opened my first brokerage account, not one person I knew traded stock. Now that professional niche activity has blown into the mainstream because people want to sit at home in their sweatpants and make money on their laptop. During the lockdowns in 2020, the whole world decided that would be a great way to fill their time.

Now, every single kid on their iPhone trading stocks at work is stealing time from their employer or, worse, wasting their parents' money. They might genuinely think that they don't need to go to work if they can trade for a living. They *know* the market's about to make them rich. And they *know* that it's going to be easier than working.

Wrong. So incredibly wrong.

Trading is much harder than simply going to work. You get out what you put in. Quick money comes and goes with no sense of satisfaction or pride, but if you work your tail off, you start to reap tangible rewards. You reap what you sow. If you don't know much about stock or crypto trading, then you have no idea that the odds of becoming a full-time trader are extraordinarily rare. It is much, much harder to carve out a living in the market than it is working for a living. Why? Because of your mind. That's why this book started with your money mind and why it's essential that you continue its journey and education.

When you trade on tips and you win, you think, "Wow, this really works." But easy come, easy go. You'll put it right back in within days on the next tip, so you lose either way. You lose if you lose, but you're going to lose if you win too. That is, if you don't know how to manage money. And how could you expect to inherently know that? It takes years of discipline to effectively manage a portfolio. It takes many years and many tax filings to learn the ins and outs of corporate and income taxes. But you'll need to know this intimately if you are to become a full-time investor.

Watch out for brokers who offer no-commission trades. Think about it. It's insane to think that you're not actually paying for the broker's service. How would they make money otherwise? The broker is simply carving his piece out of your end, just like a realtor. It's identical to the Mercedes-Benz dealership touting noncommissioned salespeople that adds $1,000 to the MSRP for administration, doc fees, or prep to pay the salesperson. The broker fills *you* at $10.45 book-value per share and fails to disclose to you that his firm's actual cost on the fill was only $10.35 per share. He—and the firm—made their commission on the spread, because no one in the markets does anything for free.

AIN'T NO SUCH THING AS HALFWAY CROOKS

Don't play with your heart and your capital until you understand fully that the house is rigged and that you are its potential prey. Gamble only within your means and your range. Try to stay within limits that have no physical consequences, such as immediate stomach pain or any lack of sleep. Far too many people are ignoring this right now, riding gut-wrenching positions and losing enough sleep to carve years off their lives. Remember that no one is looking out for your interests but you. Everyone else is too busy looking out for their own interests.

Whenever you get tips—"So-and-so is going to merge," or "I heard that there's going to be a huge promotional pump on Shiba Inu Coin"—remember this. If that information *is* true and came from inside a company, you're now acting on privileged inside information. Even if it came to you twenty hands down the line, you are an accessory to a crime if you act upon it. Acting on a tip fucks you up both ways: if it's not real, you're an idiot for listening to it. And if it is real, you're a halfway crook—that is to say, guilty of trying to front-run something, which indicates you are dumping into unsuspecting victims, who didn't know the tip. Your ill-gotten gain is their loss. On the street, that's called theft.

If you buy or sell shares because you know something other people don't, you're taking from them. It's stealing from those who don't have the privileged information that you do. Yes, this is how Wall Street, Bay Street, and Howe Street work for the most part. But no, that does not mean that you should do it too. The wealthy guy who doesn't have to break the law is so much more interesting than the greasy one that has to cut all the corners. How do you trust those people if that's their behavior? As above, so below. You can never align yourself with corner cutters because the real operators will immediately out you and exclude you.

How You Do Anything Is How You Do Everything

It can happen, because outsider trading is a whirlwind of information and emotion. Pure FOMO urges us to jump aboard whatever train happens to be leaving the station to try to catch a bit of momentum. You notice something flashing green on your screen. So you press forward. You don't care what it is; you want in.

I witness the stock-picking business every morning as I drink my coffee. I never act on it, but I get a kick out of seeing it in action. Stock pickers are shouting, "We're buying ticker ABC!" That ticker has a huge volume spike for the day because their followers all pile in, the price goes up two dollars in the next ten days, then everyone seeps back out. They rob the caravan and move on. There's a hurricane of big volume in, big volume out, and then they're gone like a ghost that never even really knew what ticker ABC did anyway. They raided the store, performed their smash-and-grab, and ran out—and nobody even took the time to find out what the store sells. It's the digital equivalent of a flash mob looting a department store without even looking up at the sign to see who they're stealing from.

Many "stock market experts" online charge exorbitant fees to thousands of individual subscribers for access to chat rooms that divvy out intraday stock tips. They'll "alert" to this ticker, sometimes alluding to it days in advance without actually dropping its name to build up hype. Then whatever illiquid penny they land on, the stock goes bananas for a few hours. Then the big guys owning these paid services back out of the name, using the incoming waves of noobs as their exit. Then they sit back in the Bahamas and extort companies to pay them massive fees to "cover their stock" and "present it to their following"—and all the while their following is unaware of this financial compensation. This kind of double-ending presents many clear conflicts of interest and is par for the course in the high seas of penny-stock and alt-coin fuckery.

Stock picking is little more than bullying of a low-expectation, unsuspecting stock. The cheesiest of newsletter writers drop weeks of tempting emails with bread crumbs on "the next big pick," while the company he's about to spam you with has already compensated him and has press releases at the ready to send out to the wire in hopes that you, the reader, will dive in. This is exactly how CNBC operates. They choose an out-of-favor or dormant stock, and jolt it to life for a quick win for themselves while leaving you, Mr. Investor, holding the bag. People pay a couple of hundred a month for a service like this—you probably do it yourself if you're paying for any now—but you ought to be aware of the conflict that exists if you pay for a newsletter from a writer who's also being paid by the company he's telling you about. It's completely legal with the proper legal disclaimers at the bottom of the letter, so long as it's fully disclosed. Most unethical things in the market are legal, and the same holds true for the opposite: most things that should be permitted are not.

Even Jim Cramer chatting it up with this or that CEO on CNBC is, by definition, a pump. They are pumping up the stock, and you are the end product, just as your eyes are the product—the engagement—for Instagram and Google to profit by selling you ads. If you are reading a stock tip in your email or in some thread or forum, know without a doubt that the pump is over and that you're about to step into the beginning of the dump cycle, thus participating in a smash-and-grab, no matter how far removed you are from the broken glass. You are one of the last looters stepping into the store several moments after the initial break-in, just before the five-o arrives and you say, "I had no idea." You're as guilty as the guy that threw the first brick into the window.

The Loss Feels So Much Worse than the Potential Win

FOMO kicks in. "Such-and-such newsletter writer is going to pump a stock! I need to jump in quick." It's a very cheap high. Be warned: the wins are tiny, but the losses hurt like hell. You chase another win because you're burning from the loss, but you're really just chasing a high to keep your system elevated. It's the exact same energy as driving quickly to the corner store before the deadline on this week's huge lottery that you were just reminded of five minutes ago and told, "Go get your ticket!" You are addicted to dopamine. The lottery ticket and its potential winnings aren't even a part of it; you are chasing the chemical that gets released with the knowledge of a 0.001 percent chance of getting something for nothing.

It's ten seconds of feel-good followed by lost time, lost mental energy, and lost capital repeated time and again, each time thinking, "It will be different this time." The definition of insanity.

Install friction points in your trading sphere to avoid pain. You have to stop yourself from falling victim to the biggest problem of all: human tendencies. You bet $5,000 and lose it, so you think, "This time, I'll bet $10,000 to offset the loss." Then you're in a $15,000 hole that you would have avoided had you protected your beginnings a bit better.

That's why FOMO news sprayed out by professional scumbags is so dangerous. It's the rust that continually corrodes the whole stock-trading business. *The Wolf of Wall Street* book and movie high-lighted another crook, Jordan Belfort, who lied to strangers and friends alike and convinced them to buy millions worth of stock that he himself was selling into them at the same time. Imagine the sheer callousness of these pirates to be able to lie to their loved ones, strangers, or themselves. This is why when both Jordan Belfort and Bernie Madoff were hauled off to prison, they were relieved. They could stop living a soulless existence and start to make restitution.

It's difficult not to jump aboard the FOMO train, which is why these stock-picking subscription services exist. It's all above board, the company looks good, the newsletter guy has got a decent record. You know you shouldn't but you go ahead—and those are the deals you get the most hurt on. Because you're being piggish, not bullish. You're trying to get more than your fair share from the trough.

"Why did you buy AMC?"

"Well, I turned on the TV one day, and I saw a twelve-year-old on CNBC saying, 'To the moon.' I wanted to be part of history, so I went ahead. I want to stick it to the man."

Okay, well, the man's in the restaurant buying an extra bottle of champagne tonight because you're paying for the party. You're the sheep getting fleeced by some anonymous wolf.

THE SAME CIRCUS, THE SAME RODEO

I've been burned on trading tips. One was a hedge position I'd held for a year betting on market volatility, which is a measure of how much trading activity is going on. The volatility index was incredibly low throughout 2019, and I hung on, because I was convinced there would be a huge market correction with the trade war with China, Trump's potential impeachment, and all sorts of things seemingly going awry. In the end, it was the coronavirus hysteria that tipped Wall Street into action, volatility rose, and I got out with $60,000 profit at a time when everyone else was panicking.

The problem was that I then listened to the news right after the sale, predicting that the blip was done.

"The worst is over."

"Tuesday's looking green after a Monday drop of more than 2 percent on the S&P."

The press called the situation "oversold," indicating that the worst was behind us. The news, made me doubt myself. So the very next day, I went short on the same index I'd been long on for a whole year. I hedged. I put my money back into VXX puts, this time betting that it was going back down. My bet was based on *fear of missing out*, not on reality.

My plan told me I was wrong. Greed told me I was right. Greed fucked me up. By the end of the day, $30,000 was gone. By the end of the week, all $75,000 worth of the put options were worthless. The following Monday, my original long position that I shortsightedly closed out only days earlier would have been worth over $1.7 million—and actually went much higher.

I'd chopped my winning position way too early, given up on a huge payout, and abandoned my plan of exiting slowly to maintain the hedge. A three-part *epic* fuck-up that was a real-life version of the horse-race gambler changing his plan at the ticket window after hundreds of hours of his own due diligence because of one guy's voice at the very last minute.

I'd been in the *perfect* position for *over a year* that would have netted me well over $1.5 million on the trade, but I let my emotions take control at the very worst moment—the last second of the play. And I got smoked on a biblical scale. If this book does anything, I hope it prevents even one person from experiencing one of these mental whipsaws during a long-term trade or investment.

Get a plan, practice it, and stick to it. Your emotion does not know how to trade.

CONVICTION CORRELATES WITH POSITIVE OUTCOME

If you want to play this game, you have to play detective. Do the due diligence. Take the notes; study them. Do the work before you buy the stock. Don't scratch an itch. Don't trade on your cell phone. Close your screen for a while after you've made your trades. If you sit there, you get itchy, and your trigger finger will make mistakes.

Use automatic stops. If I buy a stock because it's cheap, I have to know what is expensive. If it's a $10 stock that I know is overvalued at $20, I will not own that stock at $21. I make my mind up before I make the trade so I can either bracket the order or be ready with my finger near the trigger to drop a hot potato if need be. If it goes below $5, then the world has forgotten about it, and it might as well go to

$1. I set up a bracket: $5–$20. That's the ejection seat that can keep you alive even though the jet is on fire and spinning out of control.

Every single online brokerage offers alerts for investors that you can set up in minutes. You don't even need to put the order in. You can just set up an alert that texts you when a stock hits a certain price, it can then initiate and enter a market or limit order, or just be a notification so that you can do it yourself manually.

Be aware that the markets run on Eastern Time. At lunchtime and after in New York, the market is about a third as active as it is in the first few hours of trading. On the West Coast, I'm wasting my time if I watch the market after 9:30 a.m. Pacific Time. A lot of stocks trade 90 percent of their volume in the first couple of hours. My best days are always when I'm up at 5:00 a.m. to greet the market and force myself to look away after about two or three hours of the market being open.

When I say up, I mean boots on, reports read, ready to go. Not wiping sleep out of your eyes, starting from scratch, and acting on blind faith. Blind faith means you have no conviction. No conviction means you are an amateur. And if you are an amateur, you should probably be dedicating your mornings to learning the craft, not handing your capital over to market experts.

Buy on Rumors, Sell on News

You invest in a mining company that's digging for gold and everything looks good. Then when it releases its figures, indicating just how much gold is in the assay results, everyone gets out. That's even if the results are great. Investors sell on news because the catalyst has occurred. There is no more near-term catalyst on the horizon, so they take their bankroll and their ADD elsewhere. The cannabis sector in Canada sold off hard in October 2018 after legalization, which had hyped up the market for over five years leading up to the actual event. Legalization came, and now everyone who wasn't highly convicted of the cannabis trade had zero reason to stay in anymore. The growth had happened. Now it was just a slow game to try to get to profitability, and when you're looking for the next big thing, waiting for profitability in yesterday's plaything is not very stimulating for a nonconvicted roaming trader.

The conviction you have to believe is that this is your money. This is your family's money. You're a professional. When you spend money on stocks, it's your kids' future money you're converting into some company's shares today.

That's a useful way to pause a trigger finger, even if just for a day or two.

Personally, I will no longer buy anything that I'm not prepared to hold forever. Yes, forever. This is a firm rule I made for myself after losing over a million the fourth time by buying something I was not even intending to keep long-term. This is a strategy I successfully deploy as another friction point. It makes the standard answer *no* to 99 percent of the things I could potentially invest in or bet on today.

The advice I give to folks who have retired with some money and want to trade is to figure out what they love more than anything in the world and start trading it. If it goes lower, they can buy more and increase their holdings over time, using dollar-cost-averaging with the plan to keep it forever, because they really want to own this instrument or equity. On the flip side, if it goes way up, they can sell it, book the gain, feel great about a successful trade, and maybe wait for a reentry again at a lower price. Rinse and repeat! You can do this forever, and once you get good at it, you can wade in and out of your favorite company, making it your personal ATM.

There is *no* losing this way, financially or mentally.

That takes half the battle right out of the equation. It also removes 99 percent of the trash that no one should touch anyway. It also takes all the stress out of trading and makes it feel more like whether or not the stock is up or down, you are happy.

You've emotionally hedged yourself by only buying assets you're willing to hold forever.

As a quick example to better explain this method, let's say your stock is Apple:

Ten years ago, Apple was $13 a share. Today it's over ten times that per share. Could you buy and hold? Of course, but you could also buy the dips and sell the rips if you're partially retired and looking to generate income in the markets.

Let's say Apple Inc. tends to go up a dollar a week every week: on great weeks, it's up $3, and on bad weeks, it's down $2. That $1 move against your position is pure profit for the week. If you were inclined, you could, with a forever-mind caveat and mentality, jump in with your $100,000 every time the stock goes down $1 (in smaller slices) and sell it every time it goes up $2. You then reenter after a $1 pull back and exit after another $2 move up.

Yes, it's a ton of work, and it requires laser-like precision, although it's less so if you buy in tranches. But instead of the 1,000 percent gain in performance from ten years ago, you could have potentially made 10 percent a week and dramatically outperformed the stock over the course of a decade. But that's very much a job, and a hard one at that, so I mention this for those looking for market action as much as income. Perhaps you spent the last twenty-five years in procurement or were a salesperson for a large company; now you can procure and sell stock in the market as your new role and get paid much more than you used to.

But remember: even for all your experience, you still need to know everything that's been covered in this book. You need to do your homework.

Buying what you love is another powerful friction point. It acknowledges the danger of trading on momentum on tickers that you've never heard of before. If that precludes you from buying nine out of ten stocks out there, great. That's only going to help you. It says, "I'm not willing to hold those tickers, so I'm not going to buy them—I have enough self-respect and respect for my capital that I am not going to throw darts at tickers I have never even heard of." Let alone jump on a bandwagon to help promote or pump up some company that you knew nothing about a week earlier.

Protect your beginnings.

Three Things Are Enough to Keep Me Busy

Warren Buffett often gets asked, "How many stocks should you own?"

He says, "If you can't explain in two sentences or less why you bought the stock, you shouldn't own it."

My take is that if you can't spend at least an hour a week on each of your tickers, don't even consider adding more. With ten core holdings, I have to make ten one-hour calls to a CEO or investor relations person every week. Less is usually more.

I'm only in three or four various instruments or directions at once so I can focus on my three main areas, which gives me more than enough work to do.

I keep it simple, based on information, intuition, and conviction. On any given day, I'll use power in my house and vehicles, and I'll take a psilocybin microdose or recommend a colleague book themselves into a therapeutic session using the incredible forest medicine. So I can invest in both those categories from an experiential point of view, a place of deep understanding.

When oil starts going up in price every day, buy crude oil contracts in your futures account and make money every time you're at the pump.

It's one part emotional hedge, and one part high conviction.

Silver is very timely right now, in that it's a highly relied-upon commodity and a consumable one at that. Much of the silver that is mined ends up in landfills in the form of screens, phones, keyboards, and other electronics that rely on its conductivity. It is also needed for X-ray imaging, dental work, water purification, drug delivery, and circuit-board contacts. Silver pricing also tends to lay dormant for twenty or thirty years and then double in a year. At $23 today, I am certain that we are close to another one of those bull cycles,

MONEY MIND

decades in the making, that could push the important metal up past $50 per ounce. Keith Neumeyer, CEO of First Majestic Silver Corp, which is the world's largest silver-primary miner, has stated many times on the record that the actual all-in cost to get one ounce of silver from the ground to your pocket is closer to $45 today than the current spot price of $23 per ounce. There's a large arbitrage play here for those paying attention to the supply versus demand debate (now and in the future).

Conviction brings a certain level of overall peace and therefore sleep quality, and in my mind, that's a high measure of success versus missing a dollar here or there. Buy, own, and hold assets that you *know*—through your own research—have value.

If you think you're going to sit on your couch for the rest of your life, order DoorDash, watch Netflix on your Apple device, and buy stuff on Amazon, all you need to do is just buy those four stocks, sit tight, and sleep soundly as time does its magic. You're in the right place. Don't overcomplicate this. You can even start to trade around your core holdings. Buy what you know and what you will continue to contribute to in terms of their top line.

Warren Buffett had his first Coca Cola when he was ten. He looked at the bottle and thought, "I'm going to drink one of these every day for the rest of my life," so he decided to invest for that reason alone. Now he's Coca Cola's biggest shareholder. It was a highly convicted trade spanning many decades.

It's like betting on sports. A lot of people bet on Tom Brady because they hate him. It's an emotional hedge. If your team loses to Brady, at least you still make money. If your team wins, you're okay with losing your money because you beat them—it feels somehow worth it.

Insurance is a hedge. You buy it when you don't need it, hoping you never do. The premiums you pay are the cost of peace of mind.

There are ways to create shifts in perception and friction points to avoid tips and fraudsters so that you sleep soundly at night and avoid emotional roller coasters.

Be Emotionless

When I make a trade, I picture myself putting on gloves and scrubbing up like a surgeon before an operation. It's a reminder to take emotion out of the process. Surgeons don't enter the operating room laughing or anxious or overexcited. They check their plan and their equipment. They have contingencies in place. Everyone in the room knows the standard operating procedure for any system failure.

Another analogy I like is that traders are like pilots. They are system monitors who respond immediately to events. If X happens, they have a protocol for it. They don't have to make decisions in real time: they rely on checklists and manuals for every instance. They fall back on the plan and on data and facts, never on emotion.

BUSINESS IS WAR
WITHOUT THE BULLETS

Independent trading often feels like trench warfare, dodging and sending bullets down range. If you place a buy order for stock, whoever's selling it pushes their shares into your bid.

If you're waging war by yourself with millions of dollars, there's no room for emotion. You're the general. Make every move as if you have an army depending on the decisions you make. That's a far, far bigger *accountability* than your own success. Everyone looks to the general for answers when things go sideways. If he doesn't have them, he's not much of a general, and his army will unravel.

The Roman emperor Marcus Aurelius said that it's possible to turn the impediment of moving forward into the *way* of moving forward. For instance, I hate working out, but after I go work out, I feel amazing and see benefits for days after. The most uncomfortable way is often the path that gets us to where we need to be. In his 2001 book *Eat That Frog!*, Brian Tracy advances a similar idea. When you wake up in the morning, the first things you do should be the things that you absolutely *do not* want to do. After that, everything else is easy. If you go for a long run in the morning, everything else just seems easier the rest of the day. Stressful events somehow feel less stressful.

Remove Emotion

Keep emotion out of the process of trading by standing up and doing some stretches at your desk. Tip your head back and move your neck for thirty seconds. Breathe deeply and mindfully for ten breaths. When you're focused on your screen for prolonged periods, your breathing becomes shallow, and your blood oxygen level depletes. Your brain is running at about 50 percent because you don't have enough oxygen in your red blood cells to make 100 percent decisions. You make it harder on yourself by trying harder to figure those decisions out.

Whenever I'm about to make a trade, I make myself do fifteen or twenty perfect push-ups. Some of the best traders I know do push-ups in their office every day for blood flow and for grounding. You take a sixty-second reset, then you stand up, and you're ready to go. It doesn't have to be physically exerting, just enough to do the job. Music also helps, as do short walks outside. All three things can be done in minutes and will help you make better decisions.

For me, it also has the effect of limiting the amount of trades I do. At fifteen to twenty push-ups per trade, I can only do about five trades a day. It's a system that saves me from myself.

It's a friction point that has a double-positive effect.

Help eliminate fear and greed by creating friction points that stop you from doing stupid things. The trading app from your phone is a very powerful distraction, so make a rule to never trade on your cell phone if you don't have to. You could also move your account to a human broker so your orders have to go through someone else if you are compulsively losing on trades. That's built-in transparency and accountability for about $100 a trade, which can be good value for people who can't control themselves. The broker chewing his tuna sandwich on the other end of the phone exists because a lot of people need that person-to-person failsafe. There is nothing wrong with preferring someone else do it if they can be more effective than you.

You can also try limiting the time you trade. For me, that's often from when the market opens at 6:30 a.m. (PST) until about 9:00 a.m. (PST). Some of the wealthiest investors in the world only trade the first hour of the market. Some traders only play in the first minute of the day, because that's when the most juice is flowing; liquidity is highest at the opening bell and then tapers off all day. By 6:31 a.m. (PST) many market wizards are done for the day.

Once you stop trading, give yourself the freedom of the day by not compulsively watching the market. If you don't need to, there's no reason to. If your day revolves around trading, chances are you'll burn out inside of three years. You're not going to last. Build a system that will serve you and your family.

Create Accountability

No one wants something simple costing them millions. Like a cup of coffee, a beer, or a big fat joint suddenly undermining your conviction, which is what these substances do. I often joke that if the stock market were open at night, everything would look a lot different because everyone would be trading while they were drinking booze, not coffee.

If you drink too much coffee, ditch the cheap Keurig and make it a long, drawn-out ritual with a nice espresso machine or French

MONEY MIND

press, and you'll drink way less coffee while enjoying each cup more. Friction points.

It's the same with a journal. It was only when I started writing all my activities down on paper that I could get a 30,000-foot view. Simply writing a journal is thought inducing. Every time I was journaling regularly, an almost cosmic awareness would unfold itself on the page in front of me. Keeping a journal reinforces decisions and increases accountability. It helped me see the lunacy as well.

You can't bullshit yourself when you're journaling. You may bullshit yourself on the fly, but when you stop and journal, it helps you to see the forest for the trees.

All those things create accountability.

WHEN IN DOUBT, STAY OUT

Berkshire Hathaway is one of the best-performing stocks of the last fifty years. We've already seen how Warren Buffett, its president, reads fifteen newspapers a day and only allows about three stock transactions per year. Coincidence? Or proof?

The best traders never, ever chase opportunities. They do a lot of research, and they get in for all the right reasons for the very-long-term. If the Oracle of Omaha trades three times a year and you trade twenty times a day, who do you think has something to learn from the other?

Berkshire Hathaway set the benchmark for success. They trim here and there to rebalance annually, and they don't do much else with their holdings. Take a look at your trading journal. If you're like me, you trade too much. Most traders continually trade for the sake of trading.

WHERE THERE'S HISTORY, THERE IS NO MYSTERY

The best gamblers in the world aren't really gamblers at all. They're not betting on random outcomes. They bet on sure outcomes after doing significant research and paying for advice from subject-matter experts. Your journal creates your history and removes mystery. You can look into the past to see the future once you have the past written down.

There's a Big Difference between Startups and "Acquisition Entrepreneurs"

Some people want to go and create something out of nothing, which is the hardest thing you can do. Other people want to go find something that exists they can take to the next level. Elon Musk didn't start Tesla, he bought it. Everyone assumes he founded it, but in fact, he bought a Tesla and loved it but had many ideas to make the car and its manufacturer better. So he bought the company, and he made his changes. He's an example of an acquisition entrepreneur.

An acquisition entrepreneur is far more likely to succeed than someone starting from scratch.

The Basic Approach: 100 to 1

People buy stocks and companies and have no idea what the company does. This is a disease of gambling. Moon shots, get-rich-quick schemes, lottery tickets. It's all the same distraction to separate you from your money.

If you find something you like, and you want to own it, don't just go and buy it. You learn from it first. You get in lockstep with it so you understand it completely. How does it react to good news? How does it react to bad news? What's its beta, or how it performs, compared with the overall market? When are the earnings reports due? What's the street's consensus on earnings this quarter? What is the latest economic news in that industry? Are they too far leveraged in the event of a change in interest rates? Are the insiders buying or selling? Get to know the girl at the dance properly before you offer to marry her.

There's a ratio between research and buying. Mine is one hundred hours of research and one hour of buying, minimum. Maybe yours is twenty to one when you're getting ready to buy a ticker or a coin, but I've got one hundred hours of research behind me before I buy a share of anything. And then I sleep like a baby after the trade because I am so deeply academically invested in it that nobody could convince me against it. That's professional-level conviction.

The stories I've told you about losses? That was when I didn't put in my hundred hours.

Consider spending four hours a week on each holding you own. If you don't have enough hours in the week, you're holding too many stocks. You need to learn about what you're seeing, whether it's the company's Twitter feed or their reporting. Every quarter, public companies have to put out a management discussion and analysis (MD&A), which is a round table on what they actually do day to day. The best questions you could ever ask a CEO are "What are you most excited about?" and "What terrifies you right now?" The answers are in the MD&A. You don't need to know the CEO. You can see what other executives say and what they get paid. Find out what other people are saying about them on online message boards if you have to and read up on what the general consensus about them is. Are they capable business people? Do they have a track record of success? What reputation do they have in the investment world? You can literally put the word out and ask, "What do the banks think of this company?" If stockbrokers like it, that's usually just a function of volume rather than value. What do the banks think? Do any analysts cover it? And for what reason? What are the comparable companies? How much time and energy is the company putting into the analysts and researchers to raise awareness?

In a couple of hours, you can learn so much information about any stock. The tools are already accessible from your MacBook, so you don't have to pay a dime. You don't even have to pick up the phone.

The Best Traders Back-Test More than They Trade

Keep a back-testing journal, which is when you go back through your journal and run the data of what's happened in the past to test your current strategy. Good traders ask themselves, "If I would've bought it on this day, what would have happened?" They run mock scenarios to vet their own decision-making. They can see how they would have done and simmer on the outcomes. They also paper-trade when they pick a stock and follow its performance for a few weeks or months as if they had invested in it, giving them a chance to try before they buy. Or learn the stock's behavior while they're learning about the business itself.

If you don't enjoy paper trading, then you're in the markets for the wrong reasons. You're gambling because you want a winner's rush. If you enjoy paper trading, it means you enjoy the mechanics of the process. Paper trading is one of the most undervalued assets a trader has. I still paper-trade every month. If I really want to buy a particular ETF today, I write it in my journal and look back a month later and see how I would have done.

I make another note of the price and go back four weeks later. Sometimes it tells you that you're really good. Other times, it tells you that you shouldn't be a stock trader. Either way, you're learning about yourself and your abilities. If everything you buy goes down, maybe you have a timing problem. Maybe your sources of information aren't the best. Or perhaps you're buying stock off the offer near the end of the trading session after it's had three strong days.

You can use tools to paper-trade digitally, but nothing beats just writing down how much one hundred shares cost on a particular day. Go back in a month and note it again. Do that ten times in a row, and the likelihood you can step in on the eleventh month is pretty good. Anything that you repeat, you reinforce in your mind, whether it's with muscle memory or with mental memory.

By being patient with your research and taking your time, you're jumping in armed, and you're battle ready. It's another way of keeping your emotions out of trading and investing. It's easy to feel good about the choices you make when you approach them armed, prepared, and with sufficient information.

DO NOT OVERTRADE

People who trade too much don't win. It's a compulsion, like drinking too much or overeating.

Two silent killers that decimate trading accounts over time: fees and the bid-ask spread. If you buy a tech stock at $10 and then you want to sell it, but the bid is only $9, you lose 10 percent right off the bat, just by buying it too high relative to the current bid. There's always a spread between what you can buy for and what you can sell for, just as there is if you buy a new truck, then take it straight back to the lot to trade it in. The same goes for gold bullion or exchange-traded funds. They're all going to give you the wholesale price and sell it for retail. Understand the massive implications of this on stocks that have a big bid-ask spread.

When you buy stock in the open market, you're paying retail. And when you sell it back, you'll only get the current wholesale price for it. When you buy a stock, you're behind the eight ball right away, plus you have to add brokerage commission on top of that, which is often about 1 percent of the trade. The more transactions you make, the worst you'll do statistically over time. There are lots of studies that show that accounts that churn and burn always underperform compared to sleepy accounts that trade very little—as indicated at the highest level by Berkshire Hathaway. In addition, when you try to time things, you end up overtrading in general. The best traders take positions and then build on them for months and months. Yes, you can get online accounts and trade for five dollars per trade, but if your position sizes are small, it's still a relatively significant percent of your buy or sell.

HOW TO CUT THE PIE

You won't find a how-to matrix in this book for good reason: no one but yourself should tell you what percent of your money should be in cash or in bonds. We are in uncharted territory where annual inflation numbers are officially beating mutual fund performance. Investors hiding in the wrong things are losing money. I would caution you that no one should have 100 percent of their money in real estate or in Bitcoin: those are both surefire ways to get cut in half in the future. If you're young, I suggest sticking to an easy rule of 25 percent. Never allow one asset, stock, or DeFi purchase to represent more than 25 percent of the money you have available. That way, a complete wipeout of an asset will never take you down more than 25 percent, and you will have lots of time to recover. If you're above forty, I would cut the figure to 10 to 15 percent per asset type, since you might have less time before you need your assets to pay the bills.

As for what percentage to allocate to long-term investments versus speculative investments? That's also entirely up to you and your stomach. It's also determined by how comfortable you'd be if the speculative category went to zero.

Again, I'd suggest the 25 percent rule, which keeps things really simple:

Say that John has a $1,000,000 net worth, with about $250,000 of that being equity in his home. He has another $250,000 in cash equivalents at the bank in his business account in case of emergencies, and he has $250,000 with Debbie at the bank in medium-risk mutual funds (or better yet, index ETFs for less cost). What should he do with the other $250,000? Speculate of course. First educate, then test, and then speculate. How much should he break up that $250,000 into different bets? As I've already said, he should have at least three but no more than ten current bets, none of which represent more than about 25 percent of his total equity. This is an idiot-proof system.

Taxing Affairs

I mentioned much earlier in the book how my life got suddenly far more complicated once I started to make some money on the markets. One of the topics that comes up as soon as you're successful is tax. If you plan to speculate for a living, or you make more than $100,000 per year doing it, incorporate a personal holding company, as your income tax levels to the corporation will be far less than they would to you as an individual taxpayer.

Be very mindful of the difference of income taxes versus capital gains tax and how that affects you; I've had a very bad accountant show all my capital gains as income, "to be safe," which cost me far more than my fair share of taxes. I have also had neglectful accountants pool in my trading income with capital gains, possibly exposing me to penalties. It might sound academic, as long as you declare your income, but there is a big difference to the taxman. Make sure you get a good accountant.

Be mindful of double taxation, such as speculating in your corp and then sending the post-tax corporate income to yourself personally or using it to pay off personal bills. That opens you up to more income tax on those funds, creating a double-tax environment that would have been less had you done the trading in your personal name. A good tax planner can help you there.

A tax planner will show you how to take advantage of your registered accounts, such as your TFSA and RRSP (401(k) and IRA in the US). Max them out each year first, and then put some taxable gains in your name, and then your corp third. This way, you are efficient; you'll show good income personally if you ever need to verify it, say for a mortgage, and then your corporation will protect you from any further tax that tax year on any excess income which you can later dividend out to yourself, furthering tax efficiencies.

As important as speculation is against investing, so too is capital gains tax versus income tax.

If you buy $100,000 of Ethereum this year to *HODL* forever, and then you sell it next year because it went up 200 percent, that is a legitimate capital gain and is taxed as such. If you buy the same

ETH for a quick gain and sell it that month, then you'll find that it is taxed as income because it was deemed to be generated by you and your time rather than by time alone. Many have learned this the hard way, as there is nothing on earth worse than failing to remember to put aside your taxable gain until you get the bill a year later. The sticker shock can be avoided if you anticipate the future tax bill.

This is something I've seen ruin many people after their first successful year. One way you can keep things clear for the tax people, for your bookkeeper, and for your own peace of mind is to know clearly at all times what each of your investments is to you: long term, short term, small bets, forever holds. These are important differentiators.

Try the 25 percent rule. That way, the only real work you need to do is a short rebalance once or twice a year.

Manic stock traders lose money because no one can ever be right all the time. Slow, nonfrantic investors make money because they don't need to be right all the time.

As for insurance, you can make that dead simple as well (and make no mistake, it's more important than you think). Say you pass on, leaving $2 million in assets to a partner. They will have a tax bill that year upward of $500,000, sometimes more, forcing them to liquidate assets in the estate to pay it. The solution is to insure yourself for at least 25 to 50 percent of what you are worth, just in case.

Keep it simple. You'd be amazed how well it works.

WHAT TYPE OF
INVESTOR ARE YOU?

Another way to keep things simple is to realize from the outset what type of investor you are.

One of my favorite investors in the world, Anthony Deden of Edelweiss Holdings, divides investors into three categories:

Stock Renter

This is the GameStop crowd. Their attitude is, "I don't give a damn about what it is. I just want to make money. I'm here to jump aboard a high-flying stock and ride it like a rented mule." It's like renting a car. You don't care about the vehicle at all, you just want it to work long enough to get you to where you've got to go and then get it back to the agency with the wheels still on it. You don't care in any way about the outcome of the vehicle once it's out of your possession; you'll never see it again.

Investor

The investor relies on the greater fool theory. They only buy Apple stock because they believe that someone will come along down the road next month or next year who will pay more than they paid for it today. In other words, they're still price obsessed. Whether you're renting or you're investing, the price still matters to you. You need the vehicle to look, run, and appear perfectly so that it is worth as much as it can be at a future date when you go to sell or trade it in. You are married to the car emotionally, so you care about its overall health, but only because you need to be able to get as much money back out of it at a later date.

Business Owner

The third category wants to own a piece of an actual business. They buy Nike shares because they want to own 0.001 percent of Nike in their retirement account or family trust. They have zero intention of selling, and their kids will end up owning that Nike position at some point in the future. This investor is completely unconcerned with the underlying value of the asset because they are not a seller in their lifetime. This vehicle is a family heirloom that would soon be hidden away in a storage unit before it would ever be sold off to the highest bidder. *You want to own it forever.* You care deeply about it, but only because you want it to be of some value for your loved ones when you are gone. Its ownership is more important to you than its market value today.

Being a stock renter is totally fine if that's your thing. Being a stock investor, which is what most people do, is fine too. Being a part owner of the business is fine if you're serious and you want to start to build dynastic wealth or generational wealth. Deden says that when he buys, he does not care as much about what he pays as what he's buying.

It's quality over quantity, and it's not even a long-term thing: it's a forever thing. An example. Deden found that one family has made the barrels for 80 percent of all wine in France for the last four hundred years. So he took a billion dollars and bought a percent of this family business. They have no investors, which also appealed to him. They're never going to sell. They could go on for another thousand years.

In other words, you don't have to care about the price. When you file your taxes, your accountant will assign a value, but you don't really care because your value is generational on that particular investment.

When You Shift Your Mindset, What Matters Becomes Different

When you shift your mindset from being a manic time-obsessed trader to a business owner, you will be more successful. Current sales, earnings, and share price often have very little to do with the long-term viability of a business. If you look at the big picture, Boeing had no sales for a quarter after the problems with the Boeing 737 MAX (two crashed, many hundreds died), but it's still worth well over $100 billion because the US government and its customers will continue to buy a certain number of cargo and fighter jets per year, and right now Boeing is the market leader without a clear competitor who could fulfill the demand. If you're a Boeing owner, maybe you didn't sell after the horrible 737 MAX crashes because you saw them as an incredibly sad and unfortunate blip on the forever radar. If you're a renter or even a short-term investor, however, it could be devastating to your portfolio, because short-term sentiment has been skewed, and you'll likely be shaken out within six months of the negative headlines.

The German-Canadian spiritual writer Eckhart Tolle said in *The Power of Now* (1997) that, although we are human *beings*, we're too preoccupied with human *doing*. We've got it all wrong. We think our job is to *do*, but our job is to simply *be*. We should all learn to be a little more of a being and not a doing. Especially when it comes to buying and selling stock.

When you're sitting at your computer with your hand on the mouse, it's almost impossible not to make a move.

Look away. Create those friction points. Breathe, exercise, journal, come back to your screen tomorrow with a fresh outlook.

Sit back and allow the universe to show you how you should behave when your cadence is off. That's a cosmic clue to stop before you make a big mistake. Go and hop on a bike or go kayaking and get back in lockstep with the universe. When the cosmic fabric beneath us is off, we call it anxiety or depression or disease. There are lots of names, but all they mean is that you're out of harmony. No longer grounded.

They also mean that you shouldn't trade any stock, options, or crypto today.

Go Ahead and Jump...

Money is simply fuel. If you can shift your relationship to money so it becomes similar to your relationship to gasoline, then your approach to trading will be much more measured and reasonable.

Respect your money so that it can respect you back.

I want my pain and my neuroses to help people because we're all the same and we're all predictable. I've learned the consequences of not respecting money, of trading when you've absorbed negative energy from others, or you've smoked too much weed, or you've had an extra cup of coffee or too much booze the night before. There's no reason for you to have to go through the same pain.

Treat your trading as a profession, and treat your life the same way. Protect your beginnings, and you'll unlock financial *and* personal growth. You'll be amazed at the results you could unlock.

I worked a day job and traded off the side of my desk for many years. The fear of losing my guaranteed paycheck kept me at the job long after I should have been out of there. I knew my time was better spent elsewhere, but I was afraid to cut ties—afraid of the uncertainty of having three young kids and a wife to care for. I see the same dilemma in so many people who are underemployed or understimulated workers, or who work for themselves.

That's why I wrote this book: for everyone who can relate. I want to free you from your own mind, because it's the only thing holding you back. I want you to jump. I want you to take everything you've read in this book and use it to plan your route to financial independence.

Giving up an unfulfilling job, or at least working toward a solution, is the first step to freedom.

CONCLUSION

I'm not the son of some banker. I'm the opposite. I'm a very simple, blue-collar guy. No one in my family invested in equities. I was taught that kind of thing was for people way higher up the corporate ladder—people with access and people with capital.

I was taught wrong. The stock market is open to anyone who is prepared to put in the work and who can control their emotions. You don't even need money. You just need enough of a positive mindset and desire to learn how to get started. You need a set of rules and a five-dollar journal.

The market has been good to me. I didn't get into it holding the greatest hand of cards, but I used what I was dealt to the best of my ability. I got kicked around, and I am sure I will again in the future. That's the price of admission for any independent stock trader. It's a war out there, and there's no shortage of pros looking to separate you and your money.

If you decide you want to become a professional trader, you can accomplish that goal within a year. That's my offer to you. I'm living proof that anyone can overcome the upper limit problem if they change their mindset and commit themselves to putting in the required work.

My grandparents were born on farms in small rural towns, but they didn't let that limit them. They reinvented themselves. One went on to develop real estate despite being unable to read or write. The other became a pilot and war hero despite physical limitations. They could just have accepted that their old man was a farmer, and his dad before him. They could have just stayed on the farm—that was the easy route, the path of least resistance—but they both knew they were capable of so much more. All they needed was a desire to learn and one lucky break.

One of my grandfathers got sober at age fifty and thrived for another forty-seven years, claiming to not even remember the first fifty years of his life due to the alcohol and other things. My own awareness of self-destruction is very high because I reached my fork in the road when I was twenty, when my own dad dropped dead from alcoholism.

My dad was a terrible drinker. My mom met him at an AA meeting because her father was my dad's AA sponsor. Her father gave his life to sobriety while his peers drank themselves to death slowly over time because they could never get out of the self-destructive patterns.

Seeing that dichotomy as a kid did a number on me. It exposed me to my own self-destructive tendencies as well as how they manifest themselves in stock trading.

HOW I LEARNED
THE RULES

I met my wife the day my dad died, when I went over to tell an ex-girlfriend of his. If I hadn't met her, I would have kept going down the same bad path. She brought the first real oversight into my life. She was the first person I wanted to impress, and she was the first person who saw something in me when no one else did. She showed me how to live as an adult.

With no guidance other than hers, a street-kid with no money or inheritance overcame major addictions to the bottle, street drugs and pills, overcame serious car and motorcycle accidents, a lifetime of chronic depression and debilitating anxiety, and used books to break into the stock market.

If that doesn't show you that *anyone* can find wealth by putting their money to work, I don't know what does.

I started just like you. I was a young father of three, struggling with mental health issues and financial insecurity and managing a small business in a small town. On my twenty-eighth birthday, I made a choice between the paths my grandfather and father had taken.

I chose to take responsibility for my own happiness, to slow my compulsive and destructive behavior, and to stop self-medicating with whatever I could get my hands on.

That's how I was able to give up having to ever have another job again at twenty-eight, and that's how I finally learned that life is meant to be enjoyed, not endured.

I made costly mistakes on my way, but the rules I've explained can help you avoid them—not only when it comes to making money but also in keeping your head screwed on properly.

A lot of people are white-knuckling it through life. They put out fires every day and constantly respond to the world without having a clear plan of what they want and how to get it. Using what you've learned from this book, my sincere hope is that you can change that feeling in a week.

The key to success is to stop thinking about trading and speculating purely in terms of the potential payout. If all you want is a quick buck, instant gratification will keep evading you. You need to stop and think through your own process, as we saw in Part 1. You need to think about the mindsets you need to become and stay successful. As we've learned, it's crucial to protect your beginnings. You need to start things with the end in mind. Learn to reverse engineer.

Wages will make you a living, but profits are what create a lifestyle. Once your head is on straight, you can take control of your finances and put them to work for you. By turning your checkbook and brokerage account into your tool belt, you can stop trading your time for a fee and start to generate capital gains as your income.

The day you resign from your job to pursue a vision is the day you become an entrepreneur. By applying the few simple rules I've shown you, you can turn your financial picture around much faster than you think.

Trading is a zero-sum game. For every winner there is a loser. And the house always wins. The odds are so stacked against the independent investor that winning is a struggle. You can only win through hard work and dedication—and no one wins all the time. There are no shortcuts in speculating; the pros and the amateurs are all going after the same prize.

But there's good news. You don't have to be part of a tainted system to succeed. You don't need to pay penny-stock-manipulation experts for misleading tips. You will find greater success if you mute out all the noise and stick to the rules followed by some of the investors I've helped introduce you to: Warren Buffett, Ray Dalio, Anthony Deden. They're some of the best in the world, both in terms of capital gains and quality of life. What is capital without happiness?

All you need is a plan, a path, a will to succeed, a pen and pad, some focus, and some discipline.

Remember that there is nowhere to get to with this process. No one gets *too* rich. No one gets *too* free. So stop trying to get *somewhere* and enjoy the process.

ACKNOWLEDGMENTS

Some of the important people who helped me both on my journey and with this book: Nichole, Dean, Caara, Erin, Josh, Annette, Brenna, Tye and Reanna, Dan, Cheryl, Linzee, Denise, Payton, Chayse, Corey, Donnie, Jamie, Marc, and Blair. I love you guys! And a special thanks for all the help with the writing process I received from Tim, Mikey, Sarafina, Chas, Erik, Cristina, and Tara. I couldn't have done it without you.

I want to also dedicate this book and give a special acknowledgment to the late Robert (Bob) Sutton aka Gramps, April 17, 1919–August 2, 2016. "Just for Today."

THE RULES:

11-12-10

1 → PLAN YOUR TRADE AND TRADE YOUR PLAN

Have a strategy - set an entry price, and have a reason to enter.
Have a target set before you buy, and remove any emotions from your decisions.

2 → THE TREND IS YOUR FRIEND

When the market is bullish - go long. When bearish - go short. Do not buck the trend.
Be patient, have a defined process and always wait for the pivot point.

3 → FOCUS ON CAPITAL PRESERVATION

It is focus #1. Return of capital is more important than return on capital.

4 → KNOW WHEN TO CUT A LOSS

Never become an involuntary investor by holding onto a stock after its fallen.
After an order - set a stop, limiting losses to only 1% of portfolio.

5 → TAKE PROFIT WHEN THE TRADE IS GOOD

Know your exit price before you enter. Be quick to go to cash and wait for next trade.

6 → BE EMOTIONLESS - ELIMINATE FEAR & GREED

Be mechanical, make your trades surgical. It doesn't matter where the market goes.

7 → NEVER TRADE TIPS, NEWS, SPECULATION OR HYPE

Be an informed, educated trader. Trust only your own research, analysis and instinct.

8 → KEEP A TRADING JOURNAL

After I buy, write down why. After I sell, journal it in detail.
Analyze and write down what was right and what went wrong. Learn and improve!

9 → WHEN IN DOUBT, STAY OUT

Sometimes, doing nothing is the best thing to do. Don't chase - let the market come to you.

10 → DO NOT OVERTRADE

3-5 positions at a time, no more. Too many positions creates emotional decisions.
Do not trade for the sake of trading! Treat this like a business and be surgical.

242

MONEY MIND

CPSIA information can be obtained
at www.ICGtesting.com
Printed in the USA
LVHW051545280422
716896LV00001B/4